Leaders Who Lead

KATE RUSSELL

ISBN: 978-1-64467-856-5 | 978-1-64467-818-3

CONTENTS

THINGS TO KEEP IN MIND WHEN READING THIS BOOK

Thank you for reading this book. I hope you find it a valuable guide to leadership. Being a leader is one of the biggest responsibilities you will ever have. Your leadership is going to impact the lives of not only your staff and teammates but also your family and friends and their family and friends.

Most of us take a bad day at work home with us. We reflect that negative energy on the people we love the most and some of us self-medicate with drugs, alcohol, bad food or sleep. Some of us may become abusive in our home environment because it is a safe place.

As leaders, we have to take some responsibility as to how our staff or team are going to react to the fallout of the workday with their family or friends. As adults, we all have to take responsibility for our actions at home and at work; but leaders set the tone of the workplace. They are responsible for the culture.

This book is full of practical ideas for you to try in your workplace. I have developed a workbook to help you work through the information in this book. You can access this workbook online at my website, www.adelaideconflictmanagement.com.au

Please use this resource as a way to help you organise your thoughts and to highlight the areas that you identify as needing work.

Every team is a work in progress. Even the famous New Zealand All Blacks are never satisfied with their performance. They are always reviewing and improving their approach.

The other thing to know as you read this, is that I tell a lot of stories in this book. Some of them are personal stories about my life or experiences I have had. Other stories are taken from real life experiences of teams and leaders I have worked with but the names have been changed to protect the identity of the people involved.

The stories are in italics. Stories are a great and practical way to learn a lesson or to apply your learning.

I hope you enjoy my book.

LOVE

love

/lʌv/

verb

An intense feeling of deep affection.[1]

Loving your team means that you are kind, generous, humble, vulnerable, responsible, assertive, courageous and proud.

A loving leader sets boundaries and will hold people accountable. They will be clear and unwavering about their expectations.

A loving leader will make hard decisions and take responsibility for them.

A loving leader will trust their team to have the skills to do the work that they have been employed to do.

A loving leader will take responsibility for the wellbeing of the team and will not blame the team when things go wrong.

A loving leader will be a good role model.

A loving leader knows that love is not weak, fluffy, mean or cruel.

Love is powerful, authentic and genuine.

---

[1] Oxford English Dictionary

TEAM

team
/tiːm/
noun
    Two or more people working together.[2]

"Teamwork is the ability to work together towards a common vision. The ability to direct individual accomplishments towards organisational objectives. It is the fuel that allows common people to attain uncommon results"

Andrew Carnegie

There is something extraordinary about the potential of teams. At their best, teams can create outcomes that were thought impossible.

When provided with the right environment they flourish. It is a joy to be part of such a team.

It is even more exciting to lead such a team, a team that thrives.

Teams that thrive:
- have a clear vision
- have each other's backs
- deal with conflict
- are tolerant of each other's differences
- have clear boundaries
- appreciate each other
- celebrate success

---

[2] Oxford English Dictionary

- grieve when they suffer a loss
- trust each other
- share ideas
- take responsibility for the overall wellbeing of the team

PROLOGUE

When I was 23 years old I was appointed the Manager of the Parks Legal Service, a community legal centre in the north western suburbs of Adelaide, South Australia.

I managed a solicitor and a secretary. I also managed a number of volunteers, including a group of local solicitors who helped us out every week. I answered to a board of management, sat on various committees, developed and managed the budget. I applied for grants and was responsible for maintaining a good relationship with all of our stakeholders.

I wasn't a lawyer but I was good on my feet, so I developed my advocacy skills and successfully represented our clients at the Social Security Appeals Tribunal.

I had left home halfway through my last year at school because my parents recognised that I couldn't study effectively whilst they were engaged in endless arguments. I had supported myself by working in various jobs since leaving home. I went to university for a couple of years but I hadn't finished my degree because I wasn't sure what I wanted to be when I grew up.

Here I was a few years later in a leadership role. I was a baby - it was a steep learning curve.

It was probably the best job I ever had. I met and worked with some wonderful people. I had great mentors.

I have always had a keen interest in psychology, in how people tick and this role gave me the opportunity to learn and to develop my skills not only as a leader but also as a mediator, conciliator and advocate.

This was the beginning of my lifetime career in leading and managing teams and learning firsthand how to deal with conflict situations.

Since then I have managed numerous teams. I have set up and run various teams and networks. I have also produced theatre and film which requires the management of a team for a specific purpose.

But most importantly I have worked as a mediator and decision maker. I have been in the middle of very intense and sensitive disputes, disputes about people's children, their money or their rights at work. I worked with people in high levels of conflict, who are so absorbed with justice that they can't see anything beyond the dispute in that moment. People who have been prepared to lose everything in order to fight for the principle of the matter.

These people have been great teachers. They consistently demonstrated in their actions that stress plays such a huge factor in triggering conflict and makes it sometimes almost impossible to resolve that conflict.

These people also taught me the value of letting people vent and of being believed. Everyone always believes that their position is fair and reasonable. They will always want to save face in the first instance. You can only start to change their thinking when they know you will continue to listen to them and they trust you to have their back going forward and that you will help them through the process.

This book is dedicated to all the wonderful but very stressed people I have met throughout my career. Thank you for teaching me patience and kindness in a time that is fraught with pain and fear.

1   THE SUITCASE OF PAIN

I was 15 when I worked out that the men who knocked on our front door during the working week were not my Dad's friends. They were debt collectors.

That was also about the time when I put two and two together and realised that the unopened bills that I found in the old suitcase under Dad's desk had finally caught up with him.

Although they probably didn't know it, these debt collectors had an enormous impact on our family. If they were kind and considerate in the way they approached the issue of Dad's failure to pay his bills, then Dad would be okay. He would come back into the house, go into his office and all was quiet for a while.

But if they were pushy or aggressive; if the conversation left Dad feeling embarrassed, then voices would be raised during the conversation and tempers lost. Dad would retreat into his office and sometimes he would explode. Over the course of the next day or two, Dad might throw something, threaten to throw a brick at the television (one of his favourite threats) and the answer to every question would be "no".

Dad was overwhelmed with a sense of uncontrollable shame.

Dad wasn't a bad man. He didn't deliberately not pay his bills. He wasn't trying to get out of his responsibilities. He was just living in a state he would have called 'hell'.

It all started in July 1962 when my parents married. My dad was a cattle farmer with a property at Meadows and my mum was a nurse and an actress/writer. They were madly in love. I was born in March 1963 and there is a heap of photos showing the joy and excitement of my birth.

Then in 1964 when Mum was pregnant with my brother, my dad had an epiphany. He had a near death experience and he decided to become an Anglican Priest. This was a watershed moment in their lives.

Mum did not sign up to be a priest's wife. She was seeking a life away from her controlling mother. Mum had planned a life where she and Dad and their gaggle of children would be financially comfortable and she would cook for the family and the people working on the farm. She wouldn't have to go back to work as a nurse. She would be a stay-at-home-mum and she would have some space to write. In Mum's mind, the farm offered her a wonderful life.

But that was not to be.

We moved to a tiny house in Belair so that Dad could start studying at St Barnabas. We went from living a comfortable life on the farm to one of survival, limping financially from week to week.

Mum's mental health deteriorated quickly. She self-medicated with alcohol. She went back to work as a nurse out of necessity. She now had access to prescription drugs. She started stealing sedatives from patients. And if sedatives weren't available there was always Bex. My mum took the advice of 'have a cup of tea, a Bex and a good lie down' as gospel. It's just that she substituted a cup of tea with alcohol.

Despite Mum's comatose state during my childhood, she also had good days and we had good times and life was not always dark and depressing. But it was generally always pretty hard. There was never enough money and my parents were usually dealing with high levels of stress. They argued endlessly. If they weren't arguing they were often giving each other the silent treatment.

Dad was a good priest. His congregations loved him. He was energetic, a bit quirky, he brewed his own beer and he challenged his congregations all the time. He didn't accept the Gospels at face value. He educated his congregation about compassion, being assertive and taking responsibility for their actions, rather than giving God all of the credit.

And there were a number of bonuses of our dad being an Anglican priest. One of those was that we got to go to posh private schools for next to nothing. This was a really good thing because Mum was a true snob and one of her definitions of success was that all of her children (there were four of us in the end) would go to good (i.e. expensive) private schools, just like she had. Phew!

The other good thing about being the child of an Anglican Priest was the community. No matter which church Dad was in charge of, as soon as we arrived the congregation would open their arms and accept us, no matter what. It made the constant moving from church to church bearable.

And we were not your standard church family. Mum rarely went to church and she was not a member of any groups or committees - something that I think most churches expected of the priest's wife.

To be honest, it was always best that Mum didn't go to church because when she did she would start an argument as soon as she got home; she would criticise the way Dad said something or suggest that he needed to improve his vocabulary. Dad had been educated through School of the Air during his primary school years when he was living on the family's sheep station on the outskirts of Broken Hill and he attended Prince Alfred College as a boarder for his high school years. He was not an academic at school; more of a sports jock. But Dad was incredibly intelligent and he read voraciously; he just didn't have the verbal smarts like Mum. He wasn't a snob and he was a priest, something my mother really never came to terms with.

We moved a lot. That's what priest's families do. But we kids went to our stable snobby expensive private schools, so at least we didn't have to change those friendship groups all of the time.

When I was about 13 we moved to our final church at Sydney Street, Glenunga.

I can't tell you how good this was. Mum was ecstatic because we finally got a posh address. I was ecstatic because I could ride my bike to school.

Mum was better for a while after we moved to the leafy eastern suburbs. She grew up in Tusmore, just around the corner, and she felt like things had finally turned around and she was 'home'. But a lifetime of drinking at least a litre of white wine a day, smoking three packets of cigarettes a day, and taking multiple sedatives at some stage during the week was hard to give up. Life eventually drifted back to being more of the same but not quite as edgy. Despite all of this, Mum continued to work in a nursing home, usually doing night duty. She was a highly functioning alcoholic/drug addict.

Mum was an extraordinary woman. She was a brilliant actress and writer. Throughout our childhood, despite everything that was going on, she was still involved in the arts. My brother and I did a couple of shows with her which were so much fun. And every summer she would somehow find the money to ensure that we got to see the big musical in town.

She had an enormous vocabulary that she could use to raise you up in an instant or sometimes cruelly bring you down to size. She did crosswords all of the time. She would sit at the head of our dining table, drinking white wine, chain-smoking, not eating and doing crosswords. It drove Dad mad.

The rectory at Sydney Street was definitely a better experience for all of us. It wasn't perfect but it had so many positives. The house was nicer and it was a bit bigger. It had a huge old portable school building in the backyard that was a great space for us kids to hang out. It was full of Dad's rusted old tools from when he was a farmer and a heap of gear that just seemed to move from house to house with us.

My brother and I were older now and we were even more independent than we were at our old house. We were living much closer to our schools so we didn't spend so much of the day on public transport. We had good friends in the area and we were just down the road from Burnside Village. As far as we were concerned life was good.

Our two younger siblings were older too. They were easier to look after. Things were looking up.

But there were always events and incidents that would bring us back to earth. World War III could start out of the blue; or even worse when Mum and Dad seemed to be getting on really well they'd go out for dinner and come back screaming at each other. It was so predictable. We always dreaded these dinners, but we were kids, what would we know?

My siblings and I never brought friends back to our house to play. We couldn't. Our house was too stressful, too dirty, too damaged to bring people to. We didn't know what Mum would say to our friends; she often tried to embarrass us in front of others. So we went out a lot. We went to other people's houses. We looked to other people's parents for guidance and to be our role models.

And if we couldn't go out, we would speak to our friends on the phone.

It was the 1970s. We had two telephones in our house. One in the kitchen and one in Dad's office. But only one line. We were all a bit telephone obsessed.

We were all trained to answer the phone properly. I had to say "St Stephen's Rectory, Kate speaking" just in case it was a parishioner ringing to speak to Dad.

As you can imagine, privacy was an issue particularly in our teen years. My brother and I fought a lot about who would get to use the phone. There was almost a booking system.

In the 1970s, when we weren't taping songs off the radio, catching up with friends after school by phone was a priority. We were always being yelled at to "get off the phone" because someone might be trying to ring the house. No call waiting in the 1970s.

However being the eldest gave me special privileges. One of those privileges was that I was allowed to make telephone calls in Dad's office if he wasn't home. I prayed every day that Dad had a meeting down at the church after tea.

It was during these times that I was on the phone in Dad's office, snooping in all of the drawers in his desk, opening cupboards and the like that I discovered the old suitcase under his desk.

It was a bit strange that Dad would have an old suitcase under his desk, so I thought it might be one of Mum's hiding places for our Christmas presents. So I opened it. What I found in this old battered suitcase were hundreds and hundreds of unopened bills.

I was old enough to know that this wasn't right. I knew what bills looked like and I knew that the only way to know how much you had to pay was to open the envelope. But I was a teenager so I didn't think too much about it at the time.

So I went back to worrying about my important social life. I worried about making telephone contact with my friends; about what I would wear to the next plain clothes day at school which was always stressful for me because most of my clothes were hand me downs from parishioners. And I worried about what song my favourite radio station was going to play next and if I would be fast enough to tape the first few bars of the song. That was always tricky.

The penny started to drop during the summer school holidays. I was about 15 years old. A man turned up to the front door. Dad put on his formal voice; I could tell that he was embarrassed. They were talking and talking. I could hear Dad justifying why there were problems. He wasn't his usual friendly self. Dad started getting agitated. He yelled, "What do you expect me to do? I don't have the money!" and I became increasingly absorbed in the conversation from inside the house.

The conversation ended abruptly and dad tried hard not to slam the door. He stormed into his office and this time he didn't try to stop himself. Bang!

Okay. I knew what happened next. Dad was now in a rage.

I went into 'good mode'. I started to tidy up. I would do the dishes. I'd fold washing or pull out the vacuum cleaner. I worked and worked, trying to diminish the number of things Dad could complain about.

Then I warned my siblings to not upset Dad. We knew how to 'behave' when Dad was in this state, but we had no control over Mum.

Chances were strong that Dad would get very agitated that night if we were all found watching television, enjoying ourselves. Dad would be counting Mum's drinks. So Mum would hide her drink and her cigarettes on top of the fridge as if we all didn't know where she put them when Dad was in a state.

All this behaviour was very predictable. This didn't happen all of the time; but when it was on, it was on. This dark mood could last for days. During school holidays we would all just take off for the day if Dad was in a mood. Anything to not be at home.

I was also aware that there were times when Dad would have similar conversations with these people who came to our door from time to time and Dad would be okay. Dad would be formal and polite and say thank you a lot and after a relatively quiet conversation, Dad would come back inside and quietly retreat to his office.

The shame was reduced; the embarrassment manageable if Dad was treated with kindness and respect by these men, who I eventually worked out were debt collectors.

My dad's mood could turn in an instant, dramatically so, depending on the approach taken by these men who were only doing their job.

I spent my childhood being hyper-vigilant and observant in order to keep myself and my siblings safe.

I was also often expected to be a quasi-parent to my siblings because one or both of my parents weren't capable of executing their responsibilities in the moment. My dad was sometimes the scariest person I knew because he was so stressed, but I was very close to him. We were often the team. We were the ones that looked after everyone else in the house.

I knew about and witnessed things that most teenage kids don't ever have to deal with. It wasn't great at the time, but it was a great teacher. I learned so much. I watched and listened and learned about how to deal with people dealing with high levels of stress, in high levels of conflict.

Dad's suitcase of pain taught me so much. Dad tried to hide his shame in an old battered suitcase. He was incredibly embarrassed by the fact that he couldn't pay his bills.

Dad wasn't a bad person. He was a very proud and capable man. He had driven a car at nine years of age, helped manage his parents' farm during the Second World War, he played a mean game of tennis and he had the respect of his entire congregation. I am also confident that Dad loved my mum but he didn't know how to manage her mental health issues. Dad also loved all of his kids so much. He would do anything for us. He worried about us all of the time; even though at times he didn't show it.

It was like we were living in a strange alternate universe. From the outside, we were doing so well. We were living in a good suburb and the kids all attended good schools. Mum worked as a nurse and my siblings and I were all actively involved in school and church activities. From the outside, we looked like a relatively functional eastern suburbs family.

But we weren't. We were very far from functional. We were broken.

Dad not being able to pay his bills was really just the tip of the iceberg. It was really a symptom of how bad things really were behind our closed front door.

And every time he got caught out, every time a debt collector arrived at our front door, Dad had to manage that shattering, overwhelming uncontrollable shame. How he behaved after being 'caught out' once again depended on how he was treated by the debt collector.

The person exposing the pain and the shame has enormous influence in those situations.

I do not believe that people are bad. I do not believe that people behave badly or hurt each other for no reason. I do not believe that people make mistakes on purpose, or let other people down on purpose.

There is always a reason.

Dad was the leader of our family. Sometimes he was the kindest, most generous person around. We knew he had our backs. He was usually the parent we turned to when there was a problem, even if he got a bit grumpy. We adored him. And sometimes, when Dad was stressed to the max, when he was overwhelmed with shame or despair he would behave in an extremely destructive and threatening manner. In those moments we were terrified of him.

Dad taught me a lot about leadership.

2   LOVING YOUR TEAM

Leadership takes a special skill set. Some people are natural leaders, but some of us have had to learn new skills and adapt our style so that we can successfully navigate the difficult and complex waters that is human behaviour.

Leading a team is different to just managing a team. Leading means taking people with you on a journey. Managing is about the getting the job done. It focuses more on the organising of people and projects. Having good leadership skills will help you be a good manager.

Both skill sets are important. There will always be an element of management in your role as a leader.

This book will show you how to lead your team with love. Because if you want your team to thrive, if you want the very best outcomes for not only you but also your team and your organisation, then there needs to be love. You need to love your team.

I have developed a model that breaks down all of the elements that are required to build a successful thriving team.

This model has been developed from my experience as a mediator and conflict specialist with over thirty years' experience of dealing with people in high levels of conflict. I have worked not only as a manager and leader; but also as a mediator and decision maker. I have decided more than 4,000 child support disputes over a period of eighteen years and I have dealt with many teams in conflict. I have firsthand experience of both leaders and staff in all levels of pain because they don't feel appreciated or respected.

Not only am I a mediator but I have also trained as a conflict coach. I have combined my knowledge with the basic elements of mediation and Cinnie Noble's conflict coaching model[3] to create a practical guide to assist leaders to feel more confident to lead.

Mediation and conflict coaching provide us with some tools and processes that assist parties to deal with a conflict situation. Consistently, the main topics that come up in any dispute are poor communication and feeling disrespected. Part of the healing process is giving people an opportunity to be heard; truly heard and believed. It is amazing how often the parties come to mediation with a more open mindset and a willingness to sort things out on the back of the pre-mediation session where they have had an opportunity to vent and be believed.

As a result of my training and in particular as a result of my years of working with people in high levels of conflict I have developed a strong understanding of conflict. I understand how it is triggered and how it can be prevented.

Conflict in itself is not bad. It is just information. It is telling you that there is a problem. If you can get clarity as to what has caused that problem you can usually sort it out. Sometimes that information leads to great developments and improvements in processes or technology or adoption of new and more humane ideology. Don't be scared of conflict; use it.

Nevertheless, conflict - particularly toxic interpersonal conflict - where there is a risk of harm to a relationship or to your organisation, needs to be dealt with as soon as possible. Unresolved interpersonal conflict can have very significant and dire consequences for the individuals concerned and to the organisation.

If we change the way in which we approach and think about conflict and even better, if we can find ways to prevent toxic conflict occurring in the first place, then we'll save ourselves a lot of time, money and pain.

So how can we prevent toxic conflict occurring in the first place? How can we create a dynamic, engaged and connected team that can tolerate difference and be conflict resilient? How can we create a team that thrives?

First, you need to **discover** everything you can about yourself, your

---

[3] Cinnie Noble, *Conflict Management Coaching*, 2012

team and your business. You need to understand your values and needs and those of your team and the organisation, you need to get clarity about what your boundaries are, everyone's roles and responsibilities and the rules of the team. You need to have a clear and transparent understanding of how you and your team make decisions. You need to appreciate and value your team. You need to focus on and reward the behaviour you want and let slide the behaviour you don't. And you need to discover and identify how you and the team manage stress and how that stress impacts on your team.

Next, you need to **communicate** with your team. You need to learn how to listen, to stay in the moment and not automatically relate everything back to you. You need to be curious and when something goes wrong, you need to explore the reason why this has happened, rather than judge and punish, and you need to be respectful in all of your communication.

Finally, you need to learn to **trust**. You need to trust that the people you have engaged to help you will follow through, you need to let go of the reins and know that everything is going to be okay because most of the time it is going to be okay. You need to trust with both empathy and vulnerability. You need to gain perspective about your role in the team and your relationship with the team remembering that you can't create what you want to create without your team.

When you have all of these elements working together you will have a team that is engaged, connected and assertive.

But without them your team will be disengaged, meaning that productivity will be low and your business open to increased risks due to mistakes being made. Your team will not be connected which means that there will be little trust and poor communication. Again this will increase risk, particularly if people aren't speaking up when there is a problem.

Finally, without assertiveness and an ability to deal with issues when they arise, you will end up with a team that gossips and dobs on each other. You will be constantly putting out fires and consoling unhappy staff.

Loving your team and focusing on the positive will turn that all around. Your team will have each other's back. They will care for each other; they will respect each other and they will respect and love you.

Think back to your favourite teacher or your most loved mentor. They challenged you, encouraged you, gave you an opportunity to take risks and they trusted that you would be able to deal with the fallout. They got to know you and what was important to you. You felt safe with them; could tell them anything knowing that they wouldn't judge you. Be that leader and mentor.

My family is extremely important to me, as will be obvious as you read this book. I think that leading a team is like being a parent.

I want my kids to grow up to be independent thinkers and good people. I want them to succeed and develop and take risks. I don't want them to stay at home forever, I don't want to fix all of their problems, and I don't want them to be rude or disrespectful to their siblings or their peers.

When in doubt, love your team like you love your family and when you do that you will always know what to do next. It's instinctual.

3   TEAMS THAT THRIVE

You're in business to achieve great things, but you can't do it alone. To be efficient and effective you will need other people to help you fulfil your dreams. You will need a team. They may be employees, contractors or a mixture of both.

Chances are you already have a team and that's why you're reading this book, so you will already know and appreciate that you do need to make sure that you have a great team, made up of talented, productive and engaged people - people who will be a good fit with your culture.

The cliché is true. Your team is your greatest asset.

We generally value and respect our most expensive and prized assets. For example, let's talk about our cars. Most of us value our cars. We get our cars serviced. We wash our cars. We insure them. If someone accidentally spills something in our car, we clean it up straight away. If we hear a rattle or strange noise, we take it to an expert to get the car checked out. We trust our cars to perform as they are meant to most of the time. Sometimes we push them out of their comfort zone by taking them into difficult environments like up steep hills or over rocky uneven surfaces. We're really proud of our cars when they can deal with the harsh environments.

We generally look after our cars because we value them and we recognise that if we invest in our cars and maintain them that they will continue to perform at peak performance. The more expensive our car, the more effort we are likely to put into caring for them.

We need to look after our teams the way we look after our other valuable assets.

We need to invest in our teams, to listen to them when things are not going well, to trust them to be able to handle the harsh conditions and to deal with issues or mistakes straight away. We need to let our teams know how much we value them.

Because if we don't value our people, if we don't look after our team they are going to cost us a lot of money.

If people don't feel valued and appreciated they tend to be less productive, they complain a lot, and conflicts can arise.

And then we start to lose our people; sometimes our best people. They don't want to hang around in a 'toxic' environment. They will sometimes go to a job with less money if it means that they will feel valued or if there is more potential with a different employer.

And that's when things start to get really expensive.

The normal costs of maintaining your team are already high; particularly if you have salaried staff. Paying wages, on-costs, training and development costs and trying to ensure that your team is as productive as possible when they are at work is an expensive exercise.

And the cost of having to replace a staff member who resigns is huge.

In addition to any wages you need to pay at the time, you also have to cover the cost of:
- Loss of productivity for other staff who are covering for the person who has left
- Hiring a new person (advertising, the time you spend writing the advertisements, dealing with consultants etc..)
- Going through the termination process (administration, time spent dealing with exit interviews, dealing with other staff's expectations and the downtime that comes about when people are distracted by such events)
- Inducting and training a new staff member
- Low productivity in the first few months of the new person's employment

So we want to hire well and we want to keep our people because we don't want to incur all the additional costs that are associated with staff turnover.

Many of you may have accidentally found yourself in the role of leader or manager. You are great on the tools. You have risen through the ranks because you are good at what you have been trained to do and then suddenly, congratulations, you get to manage a team as well.

Or you grow your business to the point that you need to take on a staff member to do a certain job or fulfil a certain role for you. Your business grows fast and suddenly you have a team. Woohoo - your business is growing and doing so well! So why are you so tired, run down and burnt out from dealing with all of the staffing issues day in and day out?

As you have already worked out, leading a team is difficult. There are so many intricacies and variables that you have to deal with. But when it all comes together it is possibly one of the best feelings in the world.

So how do you create a team that thrives? How do we exploit the extraordinary potential within our teams?

The New Zealand All Blacks are the world's most successful sports team ever. They punch so far above their weight. You couldn't find a more productive or engaged team.

This didn't happen overnight. This has occurred over a number of decades. They have constantly evaluated their performance, analysed their relationships and reflected about all elements of their team over a long period of time.

Earlier this year I was fortunate enough to meet Daryl Gibson, coach of the Sydney Waratahs and former All Black. I asked him how often the All Blacks rehearsed the haka? I was interested because it's not their core business; it's not rugby. His answer - a lot. Ritual and finding something that makes you feel special are vital to a healthy team culture.

Positive team culture, team respect, team boundaries are all pivotal to the All Blacks constant extraordinary performance and world domination.

In his book, Legacy, *James Kerr highlights a number of key sayings that reflect this culture.*[4]

---

[4] James Kerr, *Legacy*, 2013

- *Haere taka mua, taka muri; kaua e whai*
  (Be a leader, not a follower)

- *Ehara taku toa i te toa takitahi, engari he tao takitini*
  (Any success should not be attributed to me alone; it was the work of us all)

- *Whakapuputia mai o manuka, kia kore ai e whati*
  (Cluster the branches of the manuka, so that they will not break)

- *He aha te kai o te rangatira. He korero, he korero, hekorero.*
  (What is the food of the leader? It is knowledge. It is communication)

Experience teaches us that leading a team is both incredibly rewarding and really, really hard. If it was so easy to get it right, my beloved football club, Port Adelaide, would win the flag every year. But they don't. Sometimes, despite having a truly brilliant playing group, some of the league's best coaches and a really positive attitude, they perform poorly, they lose games you think they would win and win games that you think they would lose. And part of that comes down to the competing interests that exist in all teams. Every AFL team wants to win the flag so they play in an extremely competitive space but with lots of distractions: like a history of losing to a particular team, like injured players, threats of players being bought out by other clubs, the birth of babies, the death of loved ones or the breakdown of relationships, a bit of jealousy of fellow teammates when a player is out of form, each player and coach's family history and emotional baggage. There are always so many elements to try to get right in any given team. Being successful and winning a flag is incredibly hard - which is why we value it so much.

Leading a team is not only tricky. It's hard work and you must take on a lot of responsibility. But there are some things that you can do that can make the role of leader so much easier.

I have worked with teams all of my life. I have been part of teams, managed and led teams and coached leaders of teams for most of the last thirty years. I have also mediated many complex and difficult conflict situations between individuals and amongst teams.

I have experienced the great highs of success as a leader and I have also experienced many lows. I have felt the extraordinary joy of seeing a team absolutely thrive; of the team performing at a level which well and truly exceeded the sum of its parts.

The best thing about getting older is that you get greater clarity and you get the opportunity over time to refine your skills. You get to try out different things and find out what works and what doesn't.

After years of working with individuals and teams and undertaking a lot of training, I have worked out what triggers conflict and how to manage it. I understand how to build trust and respect within a team.

I have applied my extensive experience and training in conflict management and leading teams to create a model to help other leaders create teams that thrive.

Figure 1. TEAMS THAT THRIVE MODEL

My model is useful because, once you understand it, you can easily see where the problem areas are in your team. You can very easily apply all or some of the elements and see an immediate improvement in your team's performance.

My model will help your team feel calm, give them a sense of harmony and confidence. Your team will feel valued and appreciated and they will feel that you and the rest of the team have their back.

My model will help you become a leader who leads, a leader who lets their team get on with the job; who trusts their team and lets the whole team take the credit for the success of your business.

This book will break down all the elements of the model. It will provide examples and practical tools that you can use so that you can apply the model straight away with your team.[5]

To achieve team harmony or create a team that thrives you need to first:

DISCOVER
Find out what is important for your team and work out how you tick.

Get clarity about:
- your vision and goals
- your roles and responsibilities
- what respect looks like, and
- your team rules

Appreciate your team:
- Look for people doing good things
- Say please and thank you all of the time
- Not take people for granted

Manage your stress:
- Understand how you react when you are stressed
- Understand how your team reacts when they are stressed
- Take action to reduce and manage your and the team's stress levels

---

[5] Genius model is designed and trade marked by Simon Bowen, www.modelsmethod.com

COMMUNICATE

Improve your communication skills with your team by:

Listening
- Being in the moment and focused on what is being said
- Being aware of what is not being said
- Not talking about yourself

Being curious
- Finding out what happened and why it happened instead of being judgemental
- Showing you care by exploring all of the issues and not making assumptions
- Allowing your staff to come up with answers and be part of the solution

Being vulnerable
- Sharing everything with your team, both the positive and negative
- Apologising when you have acted in a way that has had negative effects on the team
- Being open to being partly responsible for any issues that arise

TRUST

Trusting your team to be able to do the job you have engaged them for and trusting your team to tell you the truth by:

Being respectful
- Exploring what respect means for your team
- Honouring the boundaries that you agree to as a team
- Giving your team autonomy to get on with the job

Having empathy
- Understanding how you impact your team
- Being able to feel how others in the team are feeling
- Being part of the team; not above the team

Having perspective
- Recognising that you need your team possibly more than they need you
- Being aware of how your actions or lack of action may impact on individuals in your team
- Being humble

If you have a team that has great clarity and good communication you will get **ENGAGEMENT.**

You will have a team of people that want to be there and who look forward to coming to work each day. You will have a productive team.

If you have a team that has great clarity and there is a high level of trust you will get a team that **CONNECTS**.

A team that connects will share information and ideas. They will be innovative and looking for ways to improve how they do things. They will enjoy spending time together.

If you have a team that communicates well and there is a high level of trust, then your team will be **ASSERTIVE**.

You will have a team that deals with issues, that is not afraid of feedback, that is resilient.

If this is the team that you want, if you want to create a team that is engaged, connected and assertive, then read on. I provide you with a guide as to how to achieve that so that you can enjoy the benefits of a team that thrives.

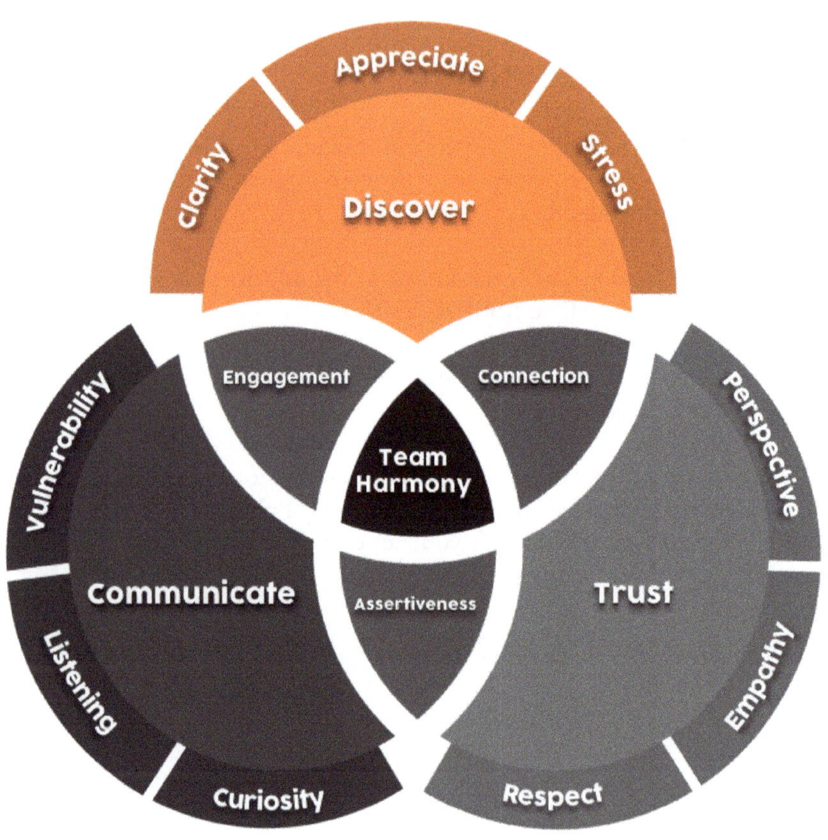
Appreciate
Clarity
Stress
Discover
Vulnerability
Engagement
Connection
Perspective
Team Harmony
Communicate
Assertiveness
Trust
Listening
Empathy
Curiosity
Respect

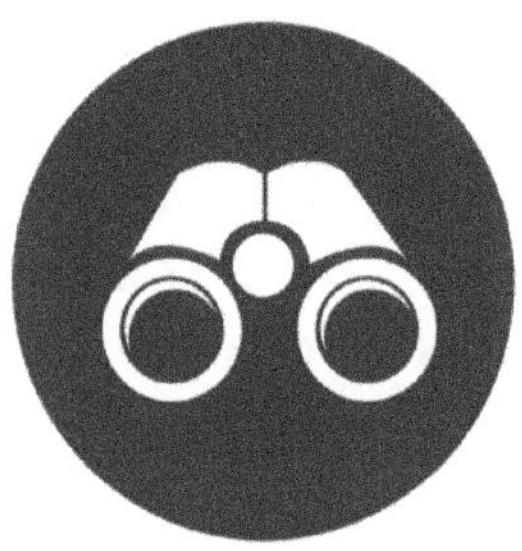

4   DISCOVER

discover
/dɪˈskʌvə/
verb
To become aware of (a fact or a situation)[6]

Recently I worked with a team that was going through a huge amount of change. Within less than twelve months this organisation had a new CEO appointed, their head office moved from Canberra to Melbourne, a number of staff made redundant and hired a lot of new staff for the Melbourne office… oh, and they had to put on a major conference!

The CEO wanted help to bring the staff from both Melbourne and Canberra offices together; to build relationships and find a way to ensure that they had a sense of team, even if they were situated over two sites.

The first step was to discover how everyone was tracking. I did this through the use of an anonymous survey. I also met with some key people to get their take on the issues at hand.

We then held a two-day workshop in a neutral venue in Melbourne. I used the results from the anonymous survey to help me determine the agenda for the workshop.

We spent Day 1 getting to know each other. Lots of fun, discovering everyone's values and needs and how we all respond to stress. On day two we got clarity. Clarity of their shared vision and goals. Clarity about people's roles and responsibilities. And I gave the Canberra team and the Melbourne team an opportunity to tell each other anything that

---

[6] Oxford English Dictionary

they believed they needed them to know.

The Canberra team expressed how they had been through a really difficult year; that the changes to the organisation had been painful and that they missed their colleagues who had been made redundant. They said that the Melbourne people didn't need to reinvent the wheel as there are already a lot of processes and practices in place; that they were open to new ways of doing things and that they had most of the corporate knowledge - so just ask if you want to know something. Finally, they said that they wanted to make this work and they wanted to work together.

The Melbourne team said that they valued the experience and skills of the Canberra team. That they knew that they were lacking a lot of corporate knowledge and they wanted to find a way to access that information without being annoying. They wanted to work together and would do whatever it took to make this work.

This conversation around getting clarity also increased the level of respect and trust between the Canberra and Melbourne camps. The Canberra team were able to safely express the grief they felt about the changes and the Melbourne team were able to show their respect for the Canberra team but at the same time raise potential issues. The teams achieved great clarity about their history, their feelings, their current roles and responsibilities and how they were going to work together going forward.

We live in an age of mindfulness. We talk about emotional intelligence. We are becoming more self-aware and this is a good thing. With greater awareness and mindfulness we have no option but to take greater responsibility for our actions and reactions to any given situation.

If we act inappropriately when we are stressed, we shouldn't be surprised when our team also starts to act out when they are stressed.

The best thing about self-awareness is that we can change the way we react to certain situations. We can get out of our own way when we recognise that we are stressed and that we are about to make a situation worse. We can also start to recognise how our behaviour might influence the way the team responds to any or all situations.

Leaders cast big shadows. What shadow do you cast?

CLARITY

clarity
/ˈklarɪti/
noun
> The quality of being certain or definite.[7]

Life gets so much easier and less stressful with clarity. It is always easier to make a decision based upon fact.

However what often happens is that if we don't know something we tend to make assumptions to fill in any gaps in our knowledge. That is always fraught with danger. Our assumptions are often wrong. We often make poor decisions based on assumptions and then have to spend valuable time and energy backpedalling and apologising.

There are many areas where you might want to get greater clarity.

- ***What is your vision?*** Is this vision shared with your team? Are you and your team all working for the same thing? Are you all rowing in the same direction?

  A shared vision is so powerful. It means you and the team can often sweat the small stuff because the energy and focus are on a much bigger prize. This in itself helps stop a lot of squabbling over relatively unimportant issues. Be clear about your vision and how you are going to achieve that vision.

- ***What are your goals?*** For you personally and for your team? Where do you want to be in three to five years? What do you need to do to get there? Is everyone on the same page? Keep track of those goals; review them. Don't let the small stuff take up most of your time when you have much bigger fish to fry. We get much greater clarity when we are focused.

- ***What are your expectations?*** Do your team know what you expect of them? Do you know what you expect of them? Can you clearly state what your expectations are? Does your team know

---

[7] Oxford English Dictionary

what your expectations are if they exceed their KPIs? Do you have a clear idea about what you expect your team will do if a big client complains or if a new team member starts with your company? Sometimes we have an idea in our head but we haven't got clarity about a certain issue and then something goes wrong and we blame our team for not managing the situation; despite the fact that we haven't been clear in the first place. Take the time to get clarity about all of this issues. Get someone to help you do a risk assessment; it will be a very valuable use of your time.

- ***Roles and responsibilities?*** Who is responsible for what? This is a really big issue for many family businesses or small businesses that grow quickly. Sometimes I have to keep asking "Who is the boss? Who is in charge?" It is not clear who ultimately has responsibility for the running of the business because the lines have become blurred over time. And you might be surprised, or not, that little things, like who is going to take the bins out each week, can cause high levels of conflict over a long period of time if there are no rules or clarity about these less popular tasks.

The other role that often needs clarity is who is in charge when the leader is not there. All teams need a leader; someone to turn to when there is a problem. If you don't anoint a 2IC, then someone will self-select for the role and that person may not be the best person for the job.

Always appoint a deputy; someone who can cover for you if you are sick, on leave, or working away. This person needs to be able to respectfully step in and out of your role; provide you with a break when you need it, be able to problem solve effectively, not get too stressed with additional responsibility and stand up when the going gets tough.

This person needs to be a team player; someone who you can trust and is respected by the rest of the team.

- ***Is favouritism an issue?*** Do you, as the leader, give some tasks to some members of your team and not others? Is it clear why you delegate work in that manner? Is this causing you problems?

Sometimes the worst performing person is deemed to be receiving special treatment.

So often an underperforming team member is deemed to be getting favourable treatment because their performance or behaviour is not being called out. It is being tolerated. The rest of the team often say to me, "Why should I bother doing the right thing, if management is going to let Bob get away with being rude to customers or turning up late every day?"

-   ***Do you have conflict in your team because they don't understand the intricacies of each other's roles or jobs?*** There are often a lot of assumptions made about why people do or don't do something. This is because they don't understand the complexities of the job at hand.

One way to manage this problem is to have a show and tell session where you get the various teams together and they get to explain in detail what their role is within the organisation. They tell everyone else some of the challenges that they are facing and they answer any questions anyone has. This is a fast way of ensuring that everyone is on the same page and will highlight where any gaps in knowledge or process are.

-   ***Are you not being told important information by your team because they are scared of how you might react?*** Is getting clarity with your team an issue for you because of your own behaviour? So many leaders are not aware of how their behaviour is impacting on their team. A stressed-out leader who is always quick to react badly to bad news is probably not going to be told a whole lot of information because it's just too scary to start that conversation.

The same is true of a leader who is hot and cold. Some leaders are like Jekyll and Hyde. They are often inconsistent, moody, volatile or the nicest person going around. Their staff are usually very wary - who are we going to be dealing with today?

We will talk about stress in more detail later in the book, but I would encourage you to start becoming aware of how you behave or react when you are very stressed? If you become a volatile tyrant, then you need to take responsibility for that and look for ways to better manage your stress levels.

Getting clarity takes time and effort. But it's worth finding out what you don't know. Knowledge is power. It helps you to make better and more informed decisions. It also speeds up the decision making process.

In saying that, some of the information you come across as you get greater clarity might be difficult to hear. You might work out that some of your staff find you intimidating or too rigid in your thinking. Try and be open-minded about everything you hear. Use it to help you be more aware as to how other people might react to you. But remember, whilst some people might have difficulty with your style, others will love it. Their feedback is information, nothing more and what you do with that information is up to you.

Learn to listen, to be open to learning more about yourself and your team. Don't punish people for taking a risk and telling you how it really is. All of this might be quite difficult to do in the first instance but the benefits will be significant. And remember your team is unlikely to give you honest feedback if they are scared that it will have negative consequences. So you are going to have to go slow and be vulnerable with your team so that they can learn that it is safe to trust you and to tell you about their experience of working with you and in your team.

This might have to be a very slow and deliberate process.

How to Get Greater Clarity

Below are some ideas about how you can start the dialogues that will give you greater clarity.

a) Regular Team Meetings

One way to start the conversation is to introduce these questions into your regular staff meetings. If you are not having a regular staff meeting, I would strongly encourage you to start the practice. They don't have to be long and drawn out but the best way for your team to have clarity is to have important conversations with everyone in the room - whether that be in person or via Zoom or Skype.

Standing meetings are the new go-to way of having a meeting. Standing keeps everyone focused and on task. No-one wants to spend more time than they have to standing around.

So what's the agenda for this meeting that is going to build clarity, trust and relationships? Well, it looks a bit like this:

Check in with everyone - how are you going?

You start with: "Good morning, everyone. Thank you for being here. I'm feeling excited for the week ahead" or "I had a pretty difficult weekend and I'm feeling a bit tired." Whatever is going on for you. Just start the ball rolling and be real in that moment.

A quick meeting of eyes and you ask, "How are you going, Bob?" And they reply. It won't take long and everyone feels included and important.

What was your number one win for the last week? What has been your main challenge?

Focus on the positive. Look for ways to celebrate wins whilst understanding what is important to your individual team members. But you don't want to get caught in the weeds here, and there will be some people who can talk under water (I know this because that would be me) so use an egg timer. Give people 3 minutes to tell you their number one win and a challenge.

The challenge will tell you where there are issues without going into a full-blown and drawn out complaint. If it is serious, you can follow it up after the meeting.

And if other people are having similar challenges you can then ask the team what suggestions they have to help deal with this challenge.

Ask them for their suggestions and then zip it - don't say anything.

Let your team come up with solutions. If they are part of the solution they will continue to look for ways to improve processes and procedures. They will also feel incredibly valued by you and the team.

What are you focusing on this week?

Check what your team are working on this week.

It's good for the team to know what everyone is focused on. It helps with problem-solving, providing additional support if it is required, highlighting if someone is trying to do too much or if they are struggling; or it might also highlight that a staff member has some spare time and could help someone else out.

Christo and Franziska from Basic Bananas talk on their podcast of a traffic light system they use.[8] They have a team that is spread out between Australia and the US. They use Zoom and their Facebook Group to stay connected with their team. Each team member has to say if their week looks like it is going to be red, orange or green. If their week is red - it means that they are feeling overwhelmed and that they could do with a bit of extra help. Orange means that it's business as usual. Green means that they have a bit of spare time and could help someone out.

This process is so useful because it gives you so much information. If someone is constantly in the red it tells you that they are not coping with the job or the type of work or that your expectations or their expectations are not realistic. You can then check what is going on with them. If someone is always in the green, you know that they can probably take on more and you can extend them more.

If someone is always in the orange it might be that they are coasting. You might want to stretch them from time to time, or mix the week up a bit.

What people are working on each week will vary from industry from industry but there is always room for improvement or to change up the focus of the week. This makes the work more interesting and this question keeps you constantly looking at ways to evaluate and improve your business or the work that you do.

Even a team that only works on a checkout or cleaning motel rooms can have something that they focus on this week. Something to aspire to or something to test out.

Always look for improvements. How can we constantly improve what and how we do whatever we do? Ask your team for suggestions. It will give you increasing clarity about your business and your team and it will build engagement amongst your team.

---

8 Basic Bananas Podcast, www.basicbananas.com/pickofthebunch

b) Planning Days

If you have an out of date vision for your company or team; or if you have never sat down and worked through this process then I would encourage you to organise a planning day.

Sometimes you need to slow down to speed up. Sometimes you have to stop and get your ducks lined up so that you progress with purpose. If you don't have a clear vision for your business, your team, or your organisation then you are going to find it hard to motivate them.

Teams that have a shared vision and shared goals are usually happier; they have a purpose and this heightens their passion. They can sweat the small stuff. They know where they are going, so it's much easier to make decisions. It's obvious who the leader is and they work with the team to achieve their goals.

Teams without a clear vision often end up arguing about small stuff. There are often various personalities with different agendas wanting to take control. The leader will find some members challenging their authority. They will push back against decisions that they don't like. It will be a constant fight while some personalities try to take control because they don't trust the leader to sort out the mess.

So whilst, it might seem that it is frivolous and time-consuming to take time out to get clarity about the big picture; the value to the team will be huge and the process will empower the leader and give everyone direction.

c) Anonymous Surveys

When a team is struggling or dealing with high levels of conflict, it can be useful to give the team members an opportunity to vent anonymously. Team members always want to be heard and they desperately need an opportunity to vent if things are not going well but they do not always feel that it is safe to speak up.

I use stakeholder engagement software, www.powernoodle.com, to conduct anonymous surveys for teams so that the leader can get more accurate feedback from their team.

I usually ask four questions:

- What do you love about your current job?

- What does it look like and feel like when things are going well?

- What does it look like and feel like when things are not going well?

- If money were no issue, what would you change about your workplace?

When this survey goes out, the team is told that everyone else is going to get an opportunity to read the results; therefore they need to be respectful.

I have access to the results before everyone else and I get them formatted in an easy to read layout.

We read the results together as a team, the CEO or manager included. Everyone is in the same boat.

I have conducted this anonymous survey multiple times and there is a trend to the way the results fall.

Firstly, the majority of people I deal with love what they do. They want to go to work because they get to use their skills or because it meets their purpose; the work is important to them. They also usually like the people they work with. It is the people and the work that is their major motivation to go to work. Not the money. I have never had anyone say that they love the money and that's what they like about their job.

Secondly, if we can capture what it feels and looks like when things are going well, then we will have a much deeper understanding of those things which create a positive culture in your workplace. You want more of that. The next step is to find ways to achieve more of that every day. We will talk about that later in this book, but knowing what makes your team happy is a great starting place for creating a wonderful culture.

The third question provides you with the problems within your team. These usually reflect problems with communication; people not feeling respected, people's work not being valued, the impact one "bad apple" might have on an organisation or the feeling that some people get special treatment. This is really useful information. So many of the complaints that come up can be addressed very easily. Don't be frightened by the answers you get to this question - this is where the gold is.

And finally, the last question gives your team an opportunity to blue sky. Sometimes the answers are so simple and so obvious but are not something that has been discussed before. This question also highlights possible problems that again once known, can be addressed.

Don't be scared of negative feedback from your team. We can only make changes for the better and improve the situation if we know what the problems are. We need to be open to all feedback; not react negatively to any criticisms and not take too much pride in the positive feedback. Keep reminding yourself - it's just information.

If you keep checking in and asking for feedback from your team they will, in due course, recognise that you are asking because you care and you want to make improvements.

I have added some added some useful tools in the workbook that will help you start these conversations with your team.

APPRECIATE

appreciate
/əˈpriːʃɪeɪt,əˈpriːsɪeɪt/
verb
> Recognise the full worth of.
>> - Be grateful for (something)[9]

Appreciation comes in at the second tier of Maslow's Hierarchy of Needs. We like to be appreciated.[10]

We like it when our efforts are recognised and we particularly like it when people notice when we have gone over and above for the good of the team.

I have heard many a leader say out loud that they don't see why they should have to thank someone for just doing their job. I think that they are missing the point.

Everyone, no matter who you are, likes to be thanked for doing a good job. Whether it is a job that you do every day or something that you do that is out of the ordinary. If someone has been "doing their job" for a long time, chances are that they rarely hear the words "thank you".

But there is something a bit magic about saying "thank you" for good deeds, big deeds, small deeds, pretty much everything. Those two words energise and engage that person. Their chest fills with pride and they feel valued and respected.

Thank you for doing your job well, without fuss, making sure that this organisation runs like a well-oiled machine, for being prompt, on time, for staying back sometimes to finish a job - whatever it is.

It's simple - always say thank you.

---

[9] Oxford English Dictionary
[10] www.psychologytoday.com/us/blog/hide-and-seek/201205/our-hierarchy-needs

Invisible Work

I have always been aware that a lot of our teammates do important and valuable work to help other people out or for the benefit of the team. It's always been something that I look for in the teams that I work with.

I didn't have a name for this work for a long time until recently when my husband, Gus, was telling me about a bit of play he had seen where Tom Rockcliff (mid-field for Port Adelaide) solidly blocked a defender to give space to the very exciting Robbie Gray (half forward and superstar for Port Adelaide) to run around and kick a goal. Gus showed me this piece of play a number of times. He said no-one would notice that Tom Rockcliff had made such a huge contribution towards this goal. It was like Tom Rockcliff was invisible.

Invisible Work is often not noticed, it's often taken for granted. So often the superstar gets all the credit but in reality, Robbie Gray probably would not have kicked that goal if not for the work of Tom Rockcliff who gave him a clear path to the goals.

The same happens in films. Having been on a number of film sets, I can tell you, there is so much work that is undertaken behind the scenes. Weeks and weeks of work before they even get to set. Long hours of setting up each of the scenes, or the people doing the actor's hair and make-up or sourcing the costumes for the production. But who gets the glory? The actors, and sometimes the director. Yet if you ever watch all of the credits, you will see that any feature film requires a large team of people working behind the scenes to make the film come together.

So I am keen to shine some light on Invisible Work, to ensure that staff or team members who go the extra mile or go out of their way to be helpful have their efforts recognised and valued.

I like to start most of my workshops by identifying the invisible work that happens in that workplace. We spend some time exploring all the things that people do that help each other. Some of the work relates to answering other people's phones, doing the dishes or cleaning out the fridge, listening to people vent after difficult client contact or bringing in treats. Some teams recognise that all their team members always pitch in to deal with small stuff, like cleaning up after an event or not being precious about who takes out the rubbish if the bin is full.

We start the process by working in pairs and then we share our ideas. We have a big sheet of butcher's paper that we record this all on and we continue to add to it for the rest of the workshop.

I always find that people keep thinking of more and more things as the day goes along. Everyone is then focused on catching other team members doing good work that usually doesn't get noticed at all. It builds a lot of engagement and connection within the team.

This is another item you can put on your regular staff meeting agendas. Get your team to nominate someone who has done some exceptional Invisible Work in the last week or month. Call it out.

Notice and appreciate the small stuff, because it's easy to see the big glamorous stuff!

Thank You Goes a Long Way

One Sunday morning in August 2017, whilst I was working away in my office in the city, catching up on some work, I received a text message from my son Tom.

Tom currently lives in Sydney where he is studying drama. He is in his second year of a three-year course.

My husband Gus and I pay for Tom's rent and most of his general living expenses; it's the only way he can live and study in Sydney.

The text said: "Hey mum. Kinda a random text but I just want to let you and Gus know that I'm honestly really grateful for all the work you both do to sustain me living here and going to the university of my dreams. I just felt like I should you know how lucky I feel that I know I can go home to a house with a bed, a laptop, kitchen, etc and none if it would be possible if it weren't for you two. Very dreary I know but I feel like I should say it more often."

After I had a little cry I rang him and asked what had happened that he felt the need to send the text. He said that sometimes he just wants to pinch himself that he is actually living in Sydney. He said it was beyond his wildest dreams that this was all happening. He had also walked past a homeless person and he realised how fortunate and privileged he was to be able to do what he wants to do. He felt the need to say thank you.

Tom's good manners and genuine need to thank people for any assistance they can offer him means that he gets on exceptionally well with lots and lots of people. Tom treats everyone he meets in the same way and they love him for it.

This is a lesson for us all. Everyone wants to feel appreciated. We want our efforts to be valued. Importantly, they want you to notice their efforts without having to remind you of the good work that they do. They don't want to be taken for granted.

And it doesn't matter how big or small those efforts are, we are constantly looking for feedback that says, "Thank you for taking the effort and time to do whatever you've done for me today."

So, look for any opportunity, at all times, to genuinely say thank you and to be gracious. And to acknowledge people's hard work and achievements no matter how small. Because they will love you for it.

People love to be thanked. They love to be acknowledged.

STRESS MANAGEMENT

stress

/strɛs/

noun

> A state of mental or emotional strain or tension resulting from adverse or demanding circumstances.[11]

management

/ˈmanɪdʒm(ə)nt/

noun

> The process of dealing with or controlling things or people.[12]

In January 2013 I went to the doctor looking for a script for a sleeping tablet. My doctor, not letting me off the hook that easily, took my blood pressure. She said I think the machine is broken and she went and got another machine.

The new machine confirmed that my blood pressure in that moment was 240 over 120. For those who are not in the health profession, that means my blood pressure was morbidly high. I was at risk of having a heart attack or stroke right there and then.

The doctor told me that I had to go straight to hospital.

I arrived at the hospital grumpy and agitated. I was self-employed and I so didn't have time to go to hospital.

They gave me a Valium. It didn't touch the sides. I was still talking at a rate of knots and incredibly agitated.

The second Valium was slightly more effective.

The doctor asked me how much alcohol I drank every day? Gulp - usually two, sometimes up to five glasses of wine per day. He harrumphed. He wrote it down.

I ended up staying in hospital for four days attached to a blood pressure cuff and a machine that went beep.

---

[11] Oxford English Dictionary
[12] Oxford English Dictionary

Fortunately, I had my computer with me, so I kept on working.

They did a number of tests to check that all my organs were still functioning properly. No-one knew how long my blood pressure had been that high for and what permanent damage I had done to myself.

On day four I was sent home with a script for blood pressure tablets and some firm advice to lose weight, drink less and exercise more.

Yep!! Sure… as if I had time for that!

In January 2014 I went back to my doctor because I couldn't sleep.

This time my doctor took some blood. This time my blood pressure was under control because I was on medication.

The results showed that my liver function test was off the scale. I was significantly overweight, drinking too much, not exercising and working at least 80 hours per week.

My doctor read me the Riot Act. He said if you don't change what you are doing you are going to die. It might not be today or tomorrow but chances are it will be in the next five years.

He sent me away with instructions not to drink any alcohol for the next three weeks; we'd see what the bloods looked like after that.

My liver function test made it look like I was drinking up to five bottles of red wine each day - impressive but not accurate. I was drinking an average of one bottle of red wine every day - sometimes more on weekends.

Every morning I would wake up with an overwhelming sense of shame. Every morning I would tell myself I am not going to drink today. Every night at 5 pm I would pour my first glass of wine.

I had every excuse in the world to drink too much. My work was hard, really hard. I did contract work for Government deciding disputes between parents in child support matters. I dealt with stressed out and traumatised people all day. I also did other work, mediating workplace disputes and helping fix workplace issues. I listened to people's problems all day every day. I also had a teenage daughter with multiple disabilities who was struggling with high school; and because I was trying to avoid all of the above, I was heavily involved in producing amateur theatre. How I managed all of this at the time is now completely beyond me, but that was what my life looked like back then.

I was so stressed. I filled every moment of every day with some form of work. Some of it paid, some of it not. The running joke amongst my family and friends was that if you needed something done, just ask a busy person. I did everything for everybody.

My down time looked like happy hour. My wonderful and patient husband would come home from work (he's in family law too) and we would have Happy Hour. He would have a beer and I would have my first (or maybe my second) glass of red for the night and we would eat peanuts and debrief the day. Often that conversation might result in a second round of drinks and more nuts and then we would have dinner. After dinner, I would take a glass of red wine into my office so that I could keep working.

So, suddenly, in January 2014, our Happy Hour ritual was thrown out the window. No alcohol for three weeks.

Oh my Lord - I was sure that this was going to be like cutting off my right arm.

Except that it wasn't.

My husband went on the journey with me. He stopped drinking too. At 5pm instead of Happy Hour we went for a walk. I was initially very unfit but very quickly my overall fitness and energy levels improved.

I decided to treat alcohol as though I was allergic to it. I also decided to change my diet at the time. In for a penny, in for a pound. I stopped eating carbs. I knew that this would work and suddenly the weight fell off me and I felt better than I had felt since forever.

I went back to the doctor after three weeks of not drinking and the blood tests showed that my liver function test results were still ridiculously high. I was referred to a specialist.

Alcohol was a significant factor but it was more than that.

The specialist told me that I had developed a fatty liver; that I have an above average risk of getting liver cancer and that I needed to lose weight, exercise and avoid alcohol in order to look after myself.

OK - I can do that.

And I did.

I pulled out of the amateur theatre, I worked fewer hours, I got a gym membership. I started running on the treadmill. Then I started running outside. I didn't eat carbs and I lost 30 kgs in eight months.

I slowly and surely got my life back.

My children suddenly noticed that I wasn't grumpy all of the time, that I got my sense of humour back. I started getting up at stupid o'clock (4:30am) and would go for a run or a bike ride until 6:30am and then I would start my working day. Now I slept like a baby every night.

I even ran a half marathon in 2015.

I disrupted myself. I changed my life around. I wish I had got the memo about twenty years ago.

I haven't had a drink since January 2014. I am not a wowser. I don't care if you drink but I can't. My liver says so. But I don't care anymore. Now I would much rather go for a walk or a run.

Stress is a normal part of life. In fact, we all need a bit of stress in our lives. It helps keep us motivated and focused at work but sometimes, we recognise that our stress levels have got out of control. And sometimes when we are very stressed over long periods of time we put ourselves at risk of ill health or accident.

Most of us are not our best selves when we are stressed. We often become increasingly self-absorbed and grumpy. We don't respond well to difficult situations. It's hard to think.

Sometimes we can hold it together all day at work but are at risk of 'kicking the cat' when we go home. Our poor family, those people we usually love the most, are the ones we often take our stress out on. At home, we might yell or have major meltdowns or we might withdraw and stop talking. Home is usually a much safer place to release the pressures of the workday.

At work, when we are really stressed we might go into micromanager mode, we might yell at staff, or be sarcastic through gritted teeth or we might lock ourselves behind closed doors and yell at anyone who interrupts us.

Sometimes, when we are really stressed at work we say things or act in ways that we very much regret the next day. This can land us in a lot of hot water. So the best thing to do, if you ever feel like you are going to really lose it at work, is to get out of there. Go to the bathroom, go outside, sit in a park, walk around the block.

Don't say or do something that you have to fix later. If you do, then apologise as soon as possible. Don't let that become an additional problem to solve later.

So what do you do when you are stressed? How do you react when you are mildly stressed? How do you react when you are very stressed? Are you aware of what you do and how your behaviour impacts on others when you are stressed?

And importantly how does your stress affect your team's performance? I suspect not very well. Chances are that your team will, when feeling really stressed, turn on each other; look to blame others and complain a lot. They will become inward focused and self-absorbed. They will feel sorry for themselves. They will take up a lot of your precious time and energy and productivity levels usually nosedive.

The good news is that stress is one area of our lives where we have some control.

The first step is to become aware of what is triggering the stress both for yourself and your team. If you know what triggers your stress, you can plan for it. Keep a diary of how you are tracking through the day.

Record what has triggered you to feel stressed. What happened in that moment, what did you do and what would you like to do differently? Be mindful of what is going on. See how your mood and behaviour impacts on your team.

By getting clarity about the issues and helping them manage their stress levels better you might immediately improve the mood of the team.

If we know what triggers us to feel stressed and if we know how we are likely to respond to stressful situations, then we can make better decisions and choices when those circumstances arise.

Managing Team Stress

I facilitate a lot of meetings for teams to identify their stress triggers. It is very cathartic for a team to be able to identify and talk about something that clearly causes them a lot of grief.

The main questions to focus on are:

- Going back over the last six to twelve months, what have been the times when the team has been most stressed?

- What were the external and internal triggers for those stressed states?

- What processes and procedures could you put in place to better manage those situations going forward?

Give your team an opportunity to identify how the stress impacts on them. Give them an opportunity to vent. People feel valued and respected if you ask for their opinion and then you listen to them. Use this exercise as an opportunity to build trust by acknowledging how difficult the last twelve months might have been.

Explore different ways on how to deal with stressful situations when they arise. Ask what they would like to see happen and get their input into solving any problems or issues that they bring up.

Finally, check in with any team members who are showing signs of stress and give them an opportunity to tell you what is going on. For example, if you see that a team member is grumpy or withdrawn, ask them about it. "Are you okay, you seem a bit grumpy?" Then be quiet; let them tell you what is going on. People will often feel relieved to have an opportunity to talk about what they are feeling; if they feel that it is safe to do so. Importantly don't breach your team member's privacy. Listen to them; give them some of your time and always ask if it is ok to talk about these issues with the rest of the team. Don't assume that because this person has trusted you with their situation that it is now information you are able to share.

Look for ways to help manage stress in your team. This will indicate to your team that you have their back and that you are looking out for them.

Don't Poke the Bear

Conflict usually occurs when we accidentally or intentionally say or do something that is at odds with the other person's personal values or needs.

For example, if I strongly value honesty and someone suggests that I have lied, I am likely to respond very strongly to that suggestion.

Our personal values and needs are very important to us. We all want to be thought of as good people.

Yet so often, when we are stressed, we say and do things that attack each other's values. We poke the bear.

Let me give you an example.

I did some work with a group of accountants.

We had been through the anonymous survey mentioned above and one of the things that most of them said in the section about what it feels like and looks like when things are not going well was that people were not pulling their weight and not working hard when they were under the pump at the end of the financial year. They were all looking out for who was working the hardest during this very stressful time.

Interestingly, the majority of those people working in that accountancy firm also all nominated 'hard-working' as one of their core values.

So when they were at their most stressed they would turn on each other, looking out for anyone not working hard. No-one could work as hard as them.

They were poking the bear. Instead of thanking everyone for working so hard and acknowledging the efforts everyone was going to, they were inadvertently looking for any examples that would confirm that everyone else in the firm was not working as hard as them.

In order to turn that around, they needed to 1) be aware of their core values, 2) give lots of praise and thank people for their hard work (or whatever the core value was for that group) and not focus energy and attention on those who were not working hard.

Focus on the behaviour you want - it will usually match the individual's core values.

Tips and Tools

Feeling stressed? Need to do something about it straight away? Here are some ideas you can implement in your workplace.

- Get out of the office and go for a walk around the block. The movement associated with walking taps into left and right brain function. It helps us think and to be creative which promotes better problem-solving.

- Make a cup of tea. Stop what you are doing and focus on a simple and rewarding task such as making a hot drink. Give yourself some space from the problem and engage in some self-care.

- Play your favourite song. Simple but effective. Get out of your head just for a few minutes and enjoy your favourite music. Personally, I would add, have a little dance here too (but that wouldn't be for everyone).

- Do something generous for someone else. Ring someone who needs to hear a friendly voice, donate some money to a cause that is important to you. Do a good deed. It helps us gain perspective when we help others needier than ourselves and it stops us being so self-absorbed.

- Do some full on physical activity - push-ups, star jumps or burpees. Again doing something that is physically taxing will help us get out of our head for a moment.

- Give someone a compliment.

AND

If you feel so stressed that you think you are going to lose your cool - just get out of that situation. Leave the building and get out.

Words said and decisions made when you are feeling so stressed that you want to lash out and hurt someone will have a disastrous impact on your team.

Sleep on the situation and deal with difficult situations a day to two days later when you are in a better and calmer state of mind.

Finally, be kind to yourself. Sometimes you will find yourself acting in a way that is not your best self; usually, because you are so stressed. Being aware of what is happening will help you deal with difficult situations better next time.

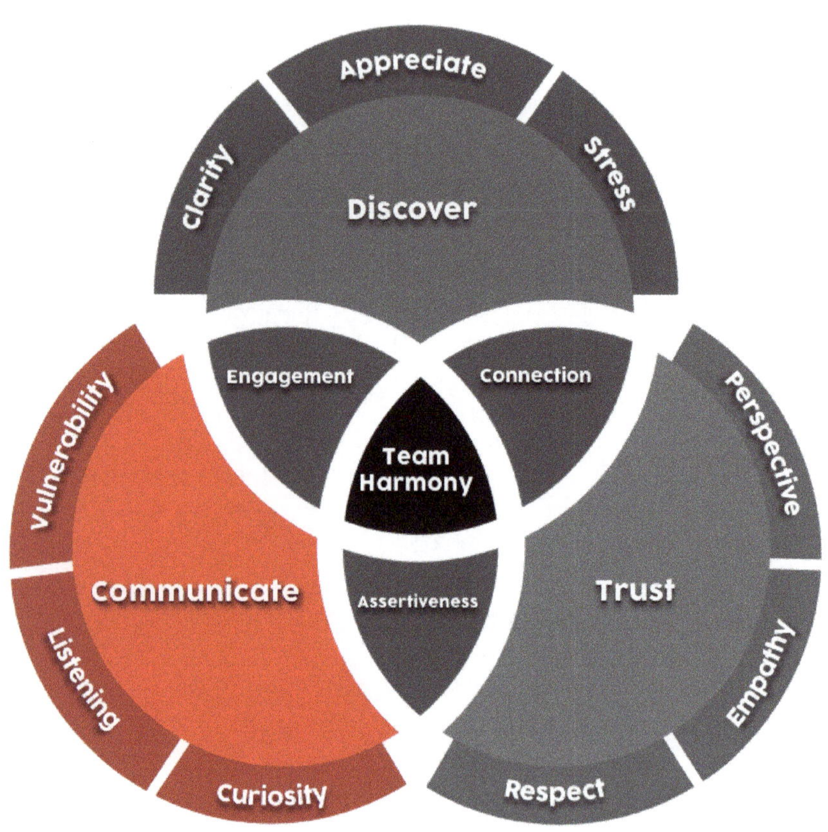

Appreciate
Clarity
Stress
Discover
Vulnerability
Engagement
Connection
Perspective
Team Harmony
Communicate
Trust
Listening
Assertiveness
Empathy
Curiosity
Respect

5   COMMUNICATE

communicate
/kəˈmjuːnɪkeɪt/
verb
>To share or exchange information, news, or ideas.[13]

The number one complaint of the majority of staff that I have ever worked with is communication, or more exactly a lack of communication.

Not communicating your expectations, miscommunication, or only some people being kept informed are some of the issues. You name it, if there is a problem in your office, someone is going to say the word "communication".

One of the problems for leaders is that you have a lot of information in your head. You know a lot of stuff; you are the one that has made most of the decisions; you usually know what is going on and what you would like to have happen. The problem is that sometimes you think others know what is in your head or you think you have explained yourself well but others have completely misinterpreted your words or they weren't listening.

As we have mentioned above, if we don't know something we will fill in the gaps with assumptions; which is usually a recipe for disaster.

So what steps can you take to improve the way you communicate? How

---

[13] Oxford English Dictionary

can you reduce the assumptions made by yourself and your team and improve everyone's understanding of everything that is important to your business or organisation?

LISTENING

listening
/ˈlɪs(ə)n/
verb
    To give one's attention to a sound.[14]

We all think we know how to listen. It's a pretty basic life skill. We listen, we talk, we converse.

Except most of us are not good at listening. Not really listening. We listen to speak rather than listen to learn.

Celeste Headlee in her TED Talk[15] provides ten important rules for improving your conversation skills. It's worth a look when you have time.

In particular, she says don't get caught in the weeds and don't be boring. She refers to the fact that our brains go faster than our mouths. We can speak up to about 150 words per minute yet we process approximately 400 words per minute. So we anticipate what the person is going to say next. We start thinking of our response; which means that we have stopped concentrating. We interrupt with witty remarks, sarcasm or a story that matches or beats the story we are listening to.

Sometimes we turn off altogether.

I have extensive experience with interviewing clients regarding their various issues. From time to time some clients go off topic. They are so grateful to have someone to vent to, they just go for it. Sometimes, if I am tired or if they have decided that they are going to tell me their life story come what may, I just let them go for it and suddenly I am thinking about what to have for dinner or what to buy my grandson for Christmas. I am not there, I have left the building.

Often when I am with family or friends, my brain is constantly thinking about a story to match the story I am hearing. My memory is triggered by someone else telling a story. I want to play that game too. I have a story

---

[14] Oxford English Dictionary
[15] www.ted.com/talks/celeste_headlee_10_ways_to_have_a_better_ conversation

too, listen to me. Suddenly it's all about me. Whoops.

As a leader, we need to listen. To be present and in the moment. We need to hear what is being said and what is not being said. We need to make it about the person we are talking with, not make the conversation about us. We want our staff and our team to feel valued and respected and to do that we need to listen to them.

I can't tell you how often people have said to me, "You are the only person who has ever truly listened to me. I feel so much better now that I have been heard."

The other thing to keep in mind is that we always want something when we speak. There is always a reason why we open our mouths. Even if we speak just to hear the sound of our own voice we do it for a reason; we do it to be heard. We often speak because we do not feel valued or respected. We want to be noticed.

Some Tips for Better Listening

When people talk to you ask yourself a couple of very important questions. What are they wanting me to know? What is the purpose of this conversation?

I have created a list of reasons why people may be talking to you as the leader.

Are they:

- **Trying to impress you** If they are trying to impress you, then they are looking for recognition and they don't think you notice them. Or they might think you have favourites (of which they are one). Or that you don't like them and they are trying to get in your good books.

- **Telling you that there is a problem** If they are telling you that there is a problem, then you need to ask, is this something that I need to deal with or should I empower them to deal with their own problem? Most people want to transfer responsibility for resolving a problem to the leader or another person.

Most people complain across or up the line in the hope that

someone else will deal with the problem; the problem is usually that someone else has done something wrong and they don't want to have a difficult conversation.

When in doubt trust them to resolve the problem. If you rescue people, they will come back for you to fix every problem after that. Do not be the person who has to fix everything; you will never get any work done.

- **Celebrating a win** If they are celebrating a win then you need to recognise that and celebrate with them. You also need to keep that information in your memory bank and make a fuss about them at the next team meeting or in front of their peers.

Remember to celebrate publicly and criticise privately.

- **Keeping you informed** If they are keeping you informed, is it something that you need to know or have you set up an environment where you need to control everything? Ask yourself, am I micromanaging this person, this team? If so, how does this benefit me and them?

Is a personal conversation about information the best use of their time and your time?

Email is a terrible communication tool but a great information tool. Use email to convey information so you have a record of it.

Speak personally to people when you need to communicate, ask questions, check something out, or when nuances are involved.

- **Sharing a joke or an interest** If you are friends and you are sharing a joke or an interest - that's fine. Just remember that you need to have these conversations with all of your staff - not just your closest friends.

Favouritism creates enormous jealousy and increases the chance of conflict. Make sure you are not seen to be having inside jokes with only a handful of staff. Share the love; find out everyone's interests and likes; get to know your team. Then you can chat with any of them at any time about things that are important to them.

Let me share an example to help demonstrate what I am talking about.

I worked with this team who worked in the health industry. They called me in because one member of the team had threatened that she would take legal action against the employer for not providing a safe work environment.

I met with the senior manager of this team. She explained that the person who made the complaint was well known to HR.

The manager was a bit embarrassed.

She said that this woman had been a problem to the organisation for 30 years. I asked what had happened now that had brought this to a head.

She said that the complainant had reacted very badly to her new team leader. The complainant had worked in an administration role within the organisation for many years and had been pretty much self-managed. But her role had changed due to the introduction of new software. In addition to this, her best friend and colleague was about to retire due to the ill health of her husband.

I was told by the senior manager that the complainant had a history of being very capable and diligent, but also rude, sarcastic and more recently not coping so well with the changes in technology.

I spoke to all the members of the broader team individually (there were seven of them) and I conducted the anonymous survey.

The complainant told me at length how competent she was; how unreasonable the current team leader was and how she didn't need a supervisor. She had a lot to get off her chest.

The team leader told me how capable she was; how reasonable her expectations were and how difficult the complainant was. She said she had no option but to micro-manage the complainant because she talked too much and didn't focus on her job. The team leader didn't really think that the complainant was up to the job any more.

The rest of the team told me about their problems, about how difficult the complainant was and most of them agreed that there was no option but for the team leader to micro-manage her.

So why did everyone tell me what they told me?

Firstly, everyone wanted to impress me. They wanted me to believe them. They didn't want to be seen as the bad person. They wanted to save face.

Everyone wanted to tell me about 'the problem' because the responsibility of the problem had been transferred to me to fix it. Everyone was keen to handball the problem away from themselves. However, when the team came back together for the group mediation, they all ended up being responsible for their behaviour and how they dealt with the problem. They couldn't truly fix the problem by handballing it to someone else.

The truth was that for thirty odd years management had turned a blind eye to the sometimes difficult behaviour of the complainant. No-one ever had ever explored why the complainant sometimes acted out; they just complained about it. However, now after years of tolerating her behaviour, she was placed in a team with a manager who openly acknowledged that she micro-managed her staff; because she didn't know of any other options.

As a leader, the most important question is *why* not *what*. Why did this happen? Why are they telling me this? Why is this person behaving in this manner? Everything happens for reason - be curious. You need to know what happened here, who is involved. You need to be curious. But then stop, review the situation. Why did this happen, why did they tell me this? Have I contributed to this situation in some way through lack of boundaries, lack of information or clarity, have I not been appreciative or engaged? Be curious; ask lots of questions. Be concerned. You might be disappointed at times and that's okay too. But remember that people do not go out of their way to make mistakes. So what is going on in your workplace that a mistake has been made?

Believe the person who is speaking - they believe what they are telling you

Finally, another lesson I have learned as a mediator and someone dealing with people in high levels of conflict is that people always believe what they are telling you - at that moment.

It may be that later down the track, when rapport is established, when there is more trust in the relationship that they will tell me something different, but in the first instance, people will always 'believe' what they are saying.

They will always justify or explain why something went wrong.

So in that moment, believe them. Go with them. Don't fight them or tell them that they are wrong. Don't start to challenge their behaviour or suggest that they are 'bad' or 'selfish' people. Just listen. Be curious and ask questions. But don't shut them down, don't argue.

Once you have a person's trust, you can then gently challenge their reasoning or help them see a situation in a different way. But if you want the conflict to spiral out of control or if you want to get someone offside, the easiest way to do this is to suggest to someone that they are telling a lie or that they are wrong.

It may be that they are lying or that they have the wrong end of the stick. It may be that they have been very selfish. But they can't tell you that they have done something wrong in the moment. It's too embarrassing, too hard, too shameful. So just accept what they are telling you at face value.

Later, they will either come and tell you more information to justify their behaviour. Or they will change their story slightly or they will be open to other reasons why something has happened. They may apologise. A whole range of things will happen, but you have maintained the relationship and you now have a chance of turning things around.

Always believe people are telling the truth; because they believe that they are. Challenging them about their version of the truth in the first instance will not be productive. Go with the flow.

CURIOSITY

curiosity
/kjʊərɪˈɒsɪti/
noun
A strong desire to know or learn something.[16]

The best first question is usually 'what happened?' – a question that helps you get your head around urgency and next steps. Ask, 'why did that happen?' Do not ask who made the mistake, 'who is responsible?' That question is loaded and generally unhelpful in the first instance.

Being curious opens our mind to new opportunities. When we jump head first into being judgemental we find ourselves in history. We can only judge others and situations from our previous experiences. But when we are curious we do not know what the answer is going to be.[17]

It's much easier to be curious when we are calm and not stressed. As soon as the situation is more serious or our stress levels are raised, the fallback position is to go into judgemental mode.

For example, you may have experienced road rage in your life. You may experience road rage every time you drive your car.

Driving a car is dangerous. It is very easy to cause harm or injury if you don't follow the road rules. If someone does something that is unexpected, like almost sideswiping us, our lizard brain goes into panic mode and we tend to immediately judge the other driver as being 'hopeless', 'an idiot', 'having got their licence in a packet of Twisties'!

The person who has accidentally almost sideswiped your car is usually very apologetic, embarrassed and falling over themselves to try to right the wrong. They already know that you have judged them as being an idiot. They feel like an idiot. We're all on the same side here - bad driving is not okay. The person who made the error is so very sorry. "I was tired, not concentrating, distracted, didn't see you etc…"

---

16 Oxford English Dictionary
17 Marilee Adams, *Change Your Questions, Change Your Life*

So the risk of injury or death makes it understandable that we might struggle with road rage from time to time. However, people making a typing error, or breaking a glass or even accidentally deleting an important document do not warrant the same reaction.

A long, long time ago, when computers were just a new thing (the early 90s), a friend and colleague and I were talking about the wonders of technology. He was showing me a document he had just completed that was all about road rules (I am not even joking) and I was showing him how to save the document on to a floppy disk or something really basic like that. We got pretty excited about basic things like saving a document back in those days.

Well, a message came up on the screen, which said something like "Do you want to save this document?" and I accidentally hit the 'no' button.

Then we both just looked at each other and realised that I had just deleted the document. Not from the disk but from the system.

We didn't have undo buttons in those days.

I looked at him and started saying "I'm sorry" over and over again. What an idiot.

He looked at me and said, "Oh my God, what have you done?"

Then he stopped and said. "That's ok, you didn't mean it. I'll take the computer to IT and get them to recover the document." (That's what you had to do in those days - take the whole hard drive to IT to recover lost documents - happened all the time).

I didn't mean to delete his document. My colleague wasn't happy (probably an understatement) but in that moment his brain went to "what can we do to recover the document" because that was going to solve the problem a whole lot better than straight out yelling at me.

Fortunately, the IT guy recovered the document and my friend and I agreed that he now knew how to save documents on to a disk and he no longer needed my help.

I make a lot of mistakes all of the time. I spill food down my front on a daily basis. I rush things. I trip over my own feet. I forget where I parked my car. I am a really big picture person so tasks that require me to focus on detail tend to go on the back burner.

I don't do those things on purpose. I do some things badly because I am human and flawed and busy and distracted.

If I am disengaged or disconnected from the group I am with, I may put in less effort to do a good job on a task or I might withdraw from a situation.

But if I am engaged and connected I will make more effort and take more pride in what I do.

If we accept the premise that we don't make mistakes on purpose, that we don't underperform just to annoy the boss, that we generally want to do the right thing, then it makes sense to be curious when something goes wrong.

Why did that happen? Is everyone okay? What is important here? What do you need in this moment? What do I need?

Look after people and ask questions. If you do that, you won't accidentally make assumptions that are usually wrong and you will be letting your team member know that you care about them. If they feel valued and appreciated by you and the rest of the team, they will go out of their way to ensure that this thing that has happened, that was a mistake or an oversight or whatever, never happens again.

It's Easy to Find Fault and to Blame

Every time there is a problem our brain goes in search of a culprit. Once we have the bad person lined up, we can deal with the issue. This 'culprit' has usually done something to someone else: been rude, disrespectful, made an error that impacted on someone else. So, we the leader, are required to do something about this terrible situation. So we take 'disciplinary action' against the wrongdoer. Phew. It's all sorted.

But it's not. Not even close.

Now you have a 'culprit' who is probably acting like a victim and you have a 'victim' who is acting like the cat that got the cream. Their relationship is shot. They are looking out for the other person to do something wrong to prove that they were right in doubting them in the first place.

This scenario, that I have seen played out over and over again, does nothing to address the real issue at hand which is usually a lack of clarity about roles and responsibilities, a breakdown in communication, or no trust between staff members. What I so often see is a judgemental knee-jerk reaction to a complex situation which probably has a lot more to do with the failings of humanity, rather than a deliberate act of defiance on behalf of the culprit.

If the 'bad person' has acted in an inappropriate manner, then the main question is why? What is going on? What would make a person behave in that manner? What are you, the leader, missing? What needs to change?

If we are curious and we explore the issue further, we might find that there are some really significant issues behind the behaviour and now that we know what they are we can deal with them.

Let's stop taking the easy option of finding someone to blame.

Let's start being curious and looking for the reason behind why something went wrong in the first place.

Let's assume that people are generally good and want to do the right thing, and then we will like them better and we won't assume the worst every time something goes wrong. Which it will.

VULNERABILITY

vulnerability
/vʌln(ə)rəˈbɪlɪti/
noun

> The quality or state of being exposed to the possibility of being attacked or harmed, either physically or emotionally.[18]

Telling your team the truth about what is going on is extremely powerful.

Many a leader has told me that they will not share bad news with their team or let them know the financial situation of the business because 1) it's none of their business or 2) they will use it against me.

If you are in this together as a team, then you need to trust that your team can cope with good news and bad news. If you are feeling scared that the business is about to fold due to a poor trading season or the like, you will be giving off vibes to your team anyway.

I always think it is better for your team to have a conversation in front of you, rather than make up facts and gossip in the car park.

If I were a team member, I would rather know that there was a problem than not know.

If you as the leader are feeling scared, angry, sad or any other significant emotion then you will display it somehow. You will be stressed and you will react the way you always do when you are stressed. You will yell at people for no reason; you will withdraw. Whatever it is, you will play your hand.

So then what happens if you don't tell your team what is going on? They will surmise, assume, fill in the gaps with their limited knowledge. If your mood is really dark over a long period of time, they might start looking for another job. They might start making decisions behind your back because you are no longer someone they feel safe with.

If you're struggling, tell your team. Tell them what is going on. They know it anyway. Operate your business or your organisation on facts.

---

[18] Oxford English Dictionary

Remember you are a team. You are connected together with a joint vision and joint goals. It's easy to share good news with the team; we made budget, we won an award, we beat our targets. It's not so easy to tell them that you have a cash flow problem, that the product is not selling well or that you don't know how to fix a certain problem.

But if you think of them as being part of the solution and not just part of the problem, you will engage them.

How much more empowered will your team be if you work through a problem together; if you fight the good fight as a team. For example, what if you had a problem with team morale after losing a big contract. You could go to your team and ask them what do you think we should do now? Asked for their input and got them to assist with the solution. What if you engaged your team as much as possible?

If a member of your family got terrible news, such as someone getting a diagnosis of cancer, then it is likely that you would share that information amongst the family, so that you could support one another through what could be a very stressful and difficult period.

Your team deserves to be kept in the loop. They need to know what is going so that everyone can have each other's backs. In order for that to happen, we have to get vulnerable. We have to share the good bits and the bad bits. We don't have to have all of the answers; we don't have to put on a brave face.

Leaders who love their teams provide leadership by setting an example of generosity, generosity of information as well as generosity of appreciation.

I have worked with lots of teams where the manager feels really uncomfortable being vulnerable in front of the team.

Yet when we have worked together for a while they usually recognise that they have inadvertently contributed to the problem. For example, they are trying to avoid confrontation so they don't deal with an issue or they recognise that they often react inappropriately and loudly when they are angry and they accidentally scare their staff.

I have witnessed firsthand these leaders apologising to the team or to some individuals in the team. They take ownership of their behaviour - for what they have or have not done. They are sincere and authentic and genuine in their apology.

Every single time, without fail, the team has reacted with love and understanding. They now get why this person has been behaving in the way that they have. The team accepts the apology and the matter is dealt with. Everyone can now move on.

Leaders do not have to be perfect; they need to be real, vulnerable and authentic.

Leading a team that is with you is so much easier than leading a team that is kept in the dark.

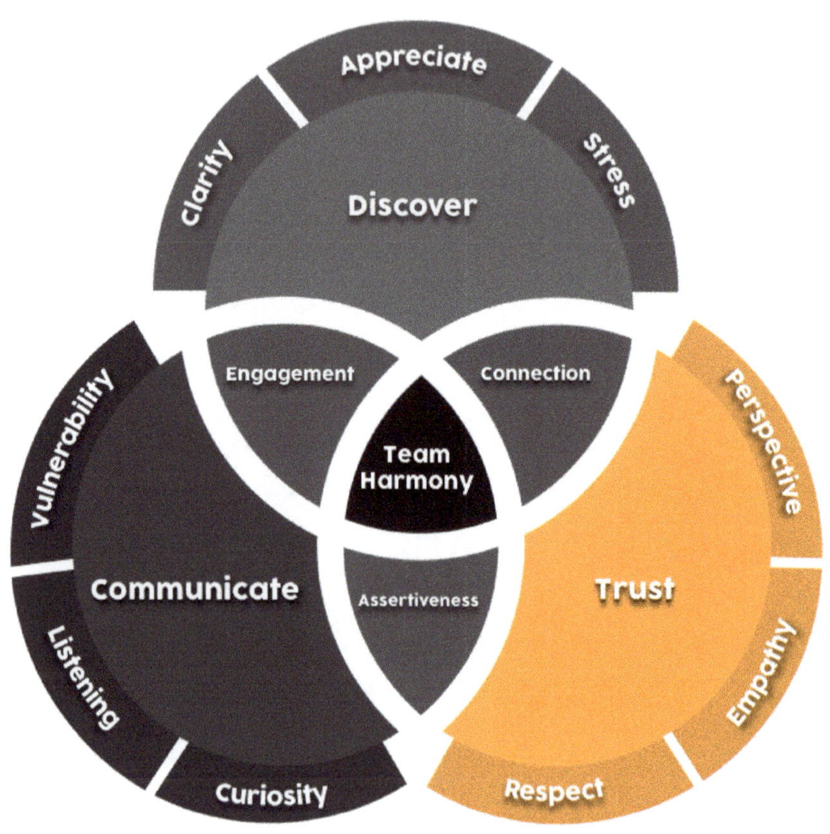

Appreciate
Clarity
Stress
Discover
Engagement
Connection
Vulnerability
Team Harmony
Perspective
Communicate
Trust
Listening
Assertiveness
Empathy
Curiosity
Respect

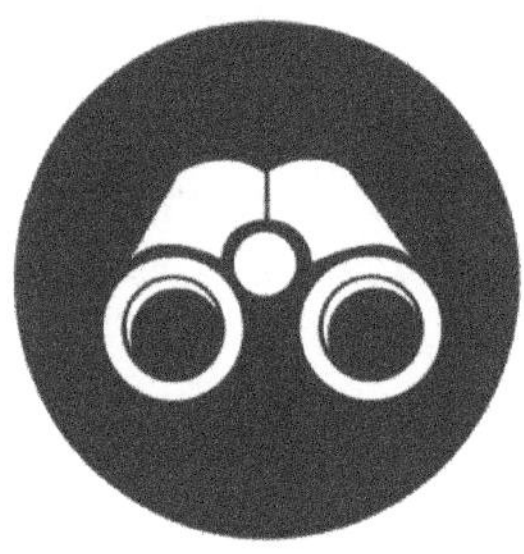

4   TRUST

trust

/trʌst/

noun

> Firm belief in the reliability, truth, or ability of someone or something.[19]

When my daughter Lucy was barely 18 years old we asked her to do a very important job for us. We asked her to look after her brother Tom, then aged 10, and be his chaperone on the set of Last Ride, the feature film he was acting in, travelling around the Flinders Ranges.

Neither my husband or I could take seven weeks off work and we needed someone who Tom loved and respected to be with him on set for the making of the film.

Lucy was a very mature young woman with a great relationship with her little brother; but chaperoning a ten-year-old on a film set when you are barely an adult with a group of strangers is another thing.

She smashed that responsibility out of the ballpark. She became an integral part of the crew. She took her responsibilities very seriously and she was awarded the respect she deserved. She was adored by all and sundry.

Tom started some days at 4 am and other days finished at 4 am. Lucy was with him all of the time. No sleep ins, no accidentally missing a deadline. Lucy had an important job to do and she did it with aplomb.

---

[19] Oxford English Dictionary

Lucy went on to chaperone Tom on other film sets. She then worked as a runner on a feature film and has produced or managed various other theatrical productions.

Trusting someone is a gift. They will make mistakes, they will not be perfect; but the more you trust, the more you will see them grow.

Trust is an antidote to fear. The other is action.

You may be like many leaders who try to control particular staff members or their teams out of fear. Usually out of fear of failure, sometimes out of fear of success.

You take the responsibility of having to achieve KPIs or meet deadlines very seriously; which is fine and reasonable. KPIs and deadlines and budgets are important. You may have invested a lot of money or time or both into a venture. You may have invested someone else's money and time into a venture.

But what often happens is that your fear of failing, of letting someone down, of losing money on the venture, or worse of losing face because you don't know quite what to do next can result in a serious case of micro-managing.

Micro-managing occurs when a leader does not trust their staff or team to do the job at hand. They look over their team's shoulder; they need to be kept informed to the nth degree about every element of every move that anyone makes. They take any feedback as criticism; they snap at people; they are stressed to the max.

Want to stop feeling so scared? Learn to trust your team. Trust the people you brought on board to do a certain job to do that job. You cannot grow and successfully develop a business if you feel you need to have control over every element of the business.

Your team will love you if you trust them.

No-one wants someone breathing down their neck 24/7 and there is a real sense of achievement when you push yourself and take risks and the risks pay off.

We also like to feel that we can work autonomously. That we can just get on and do it.

As my two-year-old grandson says when he tries out a new skill and achieves some success, "I did it!" he cries out excitedly, "I did it!"

I once worked in a solicitor's office as a secretary. Most of the lawyers were great. We'd chat about life, family and football as we made our morning coffee; they'd go out of their way to talk to the secretaries at Friday night drinks.

Sometimes they might even take some of us out for lunch or throw us a special breakfast.

But there was one lawyer, one of the partners, who locked himself in his room all day every day. He would come out to give his secretary work and then hurry back to his office. We didn't know him.

What we did know was that he was intolerant of mistakes, had a very short fuse, that he didn't seem to have a sense of humour and as a result, we were all a bit scared of him.

Sometimes in the lift, he would say hello or smile at you if you accidentally established eye contact, but I don't recall having many conversations with him.

I was a baby back then, about 21 years old. I was easily intimidated by stern older men with big impressive law degrees.

I truly wanted to do well, but I always made more mistakes when I typed up his documents than anyone else's because I did every task with a sense of dread.

I'm sure he was brilliant. I am sure that he meant no harm and that his work was very important to him. I recognised that he had a lot of responsibility in the firm to ensure that his clients were properly serviced.

But one of the things he seemed to miss was that if he wanted us to do well, to not make mistakes, to bring our best game then he needed to have a relationship with us so that he wasn't so scary. If he had a better relationship with us then he might have trusted us more and relaxed a little. If we had had a relationship we could have gone to him and asked if he could slow down a bit when he was dictating. But we were too scared to have that conversation.

So it ended up being a self-fulfilling prophecy. He appeared to doubt our abilities, to care more about his clients than his staff, and he criticised us for making mistakes.

We rewarded his lack of trust in us by making lots of mistakes and creating additional work for him.

Taking a leap of faith and suddenly trusting your staff or team may be a big jump for some of you.

But trust is a self-fulfilling prophecy, either way. The more you trust a person the more you will be rewarded. The less you trust a person, the more they will let you down.

People want to do the right thing. They want to please others.

The world is a different place since 9/11. Since that fateful day, there has been an increase in fear and the world has reacted with tighter security systems and the like. But the reality is that we are often talking about a minuscule number of people reacting to their own belief system who may cause pain and suffering for a relatively small number of people.

I am not suggesting for a moment that terrorism is not an issue or that the people affected by terrorism are not important or insignificant, but what I am saying is that our reaction to the threat is sometimes out of proportion.

Research shows that we are actually living in the safest time in all of history.[20]

And the cost of not trusting each other and of increased security is enormous. Both financially and emotionally.

But there are plenty of everyday examples where there is a lot of trust and we don't cause each other harm. For example, most of us drive on the roads every day. There are not police at every corner or speed cameras at every intersection. We are generally trusted to drive our cars in an appropriate manner. We all know the road rules (well, we're meant to) and once we pass that test we are given a licence and we can drive on any road in this country and usually any country overseas.

There is an honour system. We all know the rules and in the main, we abide by them. We might accidentally go too fast sometimes; we sometimes

---

[20] www.huffingtonpost.ca/2015/09/29/canada-election-security-safe_n_8039394.html

accidentally go through a red light because we weren't concentrating and then we usually feel very bad because we recognise the risk in running a red light.

Most of our children get through their toddler years unharmed; despite the multiple opportunities for accident or injury. The parents of a young baby who is sick or teething are usually incredibly sleep deprived and stressed to the max, but somehow we trust them to care for their child and ensure their safety.

Most people don't steal items in a shop that is left unattended; they put money on the counter or wait for the shopkeeper to come back.

There are multiple opportunities for us to do the 'wrong thing' in any given day. But we don't.

We self-regulate. We usually know the 'right thing' to do. We have societal norms that we participate in every day. We generally want to do the right thing.

The only people I know of who deliberately go out of their way to stuff something up, to destroy something or to hurt someone are people seeking revenge. Sometimes that revenge is in response to a mental health issue; which is out of that person's control.

In most situations, if you've got to the point where someone wants revenge and is prepared to do something to cause you harm, chances are your relationship is not very good and there is a history of feelings of disrespect and a lack of appreciation.

The other important element of trust is safety. Your team want to feel safe at work. They want to be able to speak up, take risks and know that they are not going to be ridiculed or yelled at.

Trust anticipates that the team is respectful at all times. That what people say will not be taken out of context in order to achieve an upper hand. That people will be empathetic, understanding and tolerant of differences.

Trust requires a fair and even playing field where the boundaries are well defined and people know what to expect. Trust loves clarity.

Trust is so important because:

- It makes your team feel valued and appreciated
- It validates why you hired your staff in the first place
- It gives your team an opportunity to play (do the things that they are good at and enjoy doing)
- You provide an opportunity for your team to take risks and to fail, which they need to do in order to grow
- It makes it safe to tell the leader that there is a problem
- It builds skills within individual team members and the team as a whole
- It builds resilience
- It reduces stress because the load is shared
- It helps your team feel engaged and creates a need for them to be connected
- Your team will feel that someone has their back all of the time
- You can't, and shouldn't, do everything

Trust is a wonderful gift that you can give to your team.

RESPECT

respect
/rɪˈspɛkt/
noun

> A feeling of deep admiration for someone or something elicited by their abilities, qualities, or achievements[21]

Teams are very demanding. They want to be appreciated, to be kept in the loop and they want to be respected.

What I have learned over a number of years is that respect is something that is quite personal. That we all have our own views on what respect means and looks like for us in our work environment.

So because people define it in so many different ways, I don't assume that I know what a person means when they say that they want to be 'respected'.

I always ask people to tell me what they mean. I have a process that I use with the teams that I work with. We workshop the concept of respect.

I get all of the team members to brainstorm what they mean by 'respect' individually; I don't want the loudest voice in the room dominating the discussion. We then discuss those ideas in pairs and later in small groups. I get people really drilling down to the intricacies of what they mean by respect. It is so important that we understand each other.

Sometimes their answers are obvious and sometimes they are not.

Some answers as to what respect looks like include:

- Being listened to
- People saying hello in the morning
- Cleaning up any mess you make
- Being trusted to do the job you were hired for
- Not emailing people after working hours
- Showing gratitude and appreciation

---

[21] Oxford English Dictionary

- Valuing an individual's skill set
- Recognising that people don't go out of their way to make mistakes
- Taking responsibility for your actions

Respect is all-encompassing. It goes to the heart of our relationships.

A team will thrive when they feel that they are respected.

If you want to ensure that your team feels respected I would strongly encourage you to find out what respect means to them.

If you do this as a group exercise, then the whole team will be aware and on the same page. You can't say you don't know that your behaviour is disrespectful if you were part of a process to identify what respect looks like and feels like for your team.

The next step for the team is to use that information to create some ground rules. Rules that the team all agree to. Boundaries for the team.

People feel safe when they know the rules and when the rules make sense and when they are adhered to.

A leader will lose a lot of respect from the team if they set guidelines and boundaries but then don't enforce those when things go awry.

A leader has to be prepared to call out behaviour that oversteps the mark.

Going back to basic principles, people don't say things without a reason and they don't act badly or inappropriately for no reason.

Everyone can always justify their behaviour; no matter how bad. If it is really bad behaviour they will tell you that they were feeling really stressed; they lashed out due to their emotion in the moment.

If it is less significant they will tell you that they were tired or not concentrating.

If you are late paying a bill; you will usually say that you overlooked the bill or you are waiting for someone to pay you and you have a cash flow problem etc. It's unlikely that you would say that you haven't paid the bill because you don't want to.

There is always a reason or an excuse. We are always looking to save face. Some people behave disrespectfully when they feel embarrassed. Sometimes we will do something "really" bad to cover for some other behaviour that is deemed even worse.

And, as discussed before, we always believe our stories. We have to. Sometimes we might backpedal once we 1) are caught out or 2) recognise that we are in a safe place and we can now relax. But in that initial moment, when we are behaving badly, we may apologise, we may tell a lie, argue, justify and usually make the situation worse because we will hold on to our initial story. But when our behaviour is called out, you can bet that we will be feeling stressed.

So remember the earlier advice:

  - When stressed get out of there and let everyone calm down; and
  - Praise in public and criticise in private.

So it depends on what the behaviour is but the first thing you need to do is check in with the person, "Are you okay because you seem really stressed?"

Just that question alone will alert the person to the fact that you have noticed that their behaviour is out of line or that something is wrong, but you are not making a judgement, you are being curious. You are just noticing that something is up.

That question will give everyone breathing space.

You can then speak with your team member privately to check what's going on or you can agree to speak to them later in the day or the next day.

It will depend on the circumstances; you will be able to judge what is the best course of action.

The number one rule is not to assume you know why the person is acting or behaving the way they are. You do not know until they tell you. So give them the space to tell you what is going on.

Ted and Mary are in a meeting together with the rest of the team. Their manager, Chris, has just announced sales targets for the next quarter. Bonuses were attached to reaching certain KPIs.

Mary's target has increased quite significantly from the last quarter; while Ted's target has reduced.

Someone in the team made a joke about Ted getting old and not being up to it anymore, and someone else suggested that Mary was the golden girl and Chris' favourite. There was lots of laughter at Ted and Mary's expense and Ted, in particular, got snarky with everyone.

Chris told everyone to calm down; that it was none of their business and that Ted was dealing with a private matter and it wasn't going to be discussed any further.

Everyone looked embarrassed and stopped talking and Chris tried to get the meeting back on track.

Ted spent the rest of the meeting smouldering and Mary looked distracted.

After the meeting, Chris found Ted and said you shouldn't let them upset you. They're just having a bit of fun.

Ted fumed at Chris, "I'm not angry at them, I am angry at you. You've told the group my targets have been reduced because of a personal matter and made it sound like a big deal. Why didn't you discuss this with me and Mary before you told the group? You know that they get jealous over stupid stuff."

What had happened is that Mary had asked for some additional work this quarter because she was planning a surprise trip to visit her daughter overseas in the next quarter and she wanted to earn some additional spending money; so Ted had offered for Mary to cover some of his areas because he wanted to go part-time for the next quarter because his girlfriend had just arrived from overseas.

Ted already felt like he was the butt of everyone's jokes, he didn't want to add fuel to the flames by talking about his private life.

Chris had not discussed with Ted and Mary how he would explain this arrangement to the rest of the team.

Chris didn't quite know how to tell the team that he had given Mary the additional work. He didn't want to have to answer those questions. Mary was his wife's best friend and there was always gossip that she got special treatment due to Chris' relationship with Mary and her family.

Chris had, inadvertently, escalated the level of disharmony amongst his team by being disrespectful to not only Ted and Mary but also the rest of the team; he was showing favouritism to Mary and there was no transparency to his decision-making process. So everyone left the meeting feeling bad.

EMPATHY

empathy
/ˈɛmpəθi/
noun
> The ability to understand and share the feelings of another.[22]

A long time ago, there was an unfortunate incident when I was managing the Parks Legal Service.

In my role as manager, I also triaged new clients. So I would either help them out there and then or refer them to our in-house solicitor or to a different agency.

I got to meet a lot of wonderful people who lived around the area.

One day a client named Ian turned up. He was about 40 years old and 6 foot 4 inches, in the old money. He seemed to have an intellectual disability. He was reliant on Centrelink payments and he arrived for his appointment carrying a plastic bag full of metal bits that clanged loudly as he walked.

I invited him into my office and asked him how I could help him. He told me that he was very upset because the oven was not clean when he moved into his new unit. He had moved into a Housing Trust unit in the local area.

I made the appropriate "that's terrible" noises and then said, so would you like me to contact the Housing Trust and ask them to come around and clean the oven? No, Ian replied emphatically. No, I wanted the oven to be clean when I moved in.

Would you like to apply for some compensation to cover the costs you have incurred in cleaning the oven yourself? No, Ian replied emphatically. I wanted the oven to be clean when I moved in.

My brain was racing by now. How could I help Ian when all he wanted was for someone to turn back time and ensure his oven was clean before he moved in?

Ian started pulling out parts of his oven from his plastic bag. There in front of me were all these metal pipes and oven bits sitting on my desk.

---

[22] Oxford English Dictionary

I asked Ian, "How do you think I can help you?"

He said, "I wanted the oven to be clean when I moved in."

I said, "But you have moved in, so I am not sure what we can do to help you."

Ian got very agitated at this ridiculous statement. He stood up, all 6 foot 4 of him. He yelled very loudly, "I want to speak to the manager!".

I stood up, all 5 foot 4 of me (with my permed hair and big padded shoulder pads - it was the 80s). "I am the manager," I said firmly, trying to look powerful and like a manager.

Ian laughed at me. He boomed "I want to speak to the manager," wielding a piece of stove pipe at me.

At this moment, the door flung open. My secretary who was also about 6 foot tall was standing there, now flanked by two security officers. Poor Ian was forcibly removed from my office and I pretended that I was okay.

I felt so bad after Ian left the building. That whole scenario was my fault.

1) I wasn't empathetic at all. I was self-absorbed. It was all about me. I was going to be the hero and fix the problem.

2) I didn't listen to Ian. What I later learned and could have deduced if I had been curious was that Ian had just moved into a new unit because his mother had recently died. He was really stressed. Ian suffered from epilepsy and his mother had protected him from the world since he was a little boy. Now he had to manage the world on his own. He was scared, lonely, confused and didn't understand how the world worked. I didn't help because I asked the wrong questions.

3) I was stressed because I didn't know how to fix Ian's problems, so I became more self-centred as the appointment went on. I was also feeling incredibly vulnerable because Ian was so tall and potentially had a weapon; my brain was spinning but I was trying to be tough at the same time.

This was a huge lesson for me. It taught me so much. I continued to make mistakes and mess up. I continued to go into saintly helping mode from time to time, but I learnt to listen and to be curious and now people tell me their life stories without me even asking. True!

Empathy is one of the tools of the trade of a mediator. We spend a lot of time getting the parties to be able to step into each other's shoes. It's hard to resolve a dispute where there is no empathy. Without empathy, we just have right and wrong.

Mediators have a "trick" to try to move people into a more empathetic state. If a person is "stuck", we ask them, if I were a stranger in a helicopter looking in on this situation, what would we see, what would we be thinking?

Sometimes people can get a different perspective and a sense of empathy if they get into the position of a non-involved third party.

But it doesn't always work and the reason for that is that when a person is very stressed, when they feel that they are under attack or that they are very vulnerable, they will go into self-protection mode. The World of One. The world of me.

We all know that world. We all go there sometimes. But some people live there pretty much all of the time.

The World of One is where you can only see the world from your eyes. Chances are you are not very generous because you can't afford to be. Usually, something has happened in your history which makes trust and empathy just too hard; it is too risky to be vulnerable, to be generous.

My daughter Georgie has Asperger's. When she has a meltdown, the only person in the world is her. All the bad things happen to her. She can only talk about her history, her problems, how unfair the world is to her. And when she recovers from the meltdown, she can be generous and compassionate and kind. But there is no generosity or kindness when she is in the World of One.

If ever you feel yourself becoming a victim, if suddenly the world is bad and you are the only person in the world that bad things happen to, then you have slipped into the World of One.

Leaders cannot be in the World of One. You cannot lead from that position. You have responsibilities to your team; they need you to be empathetic, generous and to have perspective. You can't afford to stay in a victim state.

So how do you get out of it?

- **You are aware of it, so that's a good start.**

- **Take yourself out of the situation because chances are you will make the situation worse.** You need to go for a walk or a drive but do not stay with the team because you may say or do something that you will later regret. If you can't do that, tell your team that you are not feeling very well at the moment and remove yourself from a group situation.

- **Walk fast, run or do something really physical.** The movement will help you change your mood. Do something that makes you puff and sweat. It's extraordinary how very physical movement can help you clear your mind and think more creatively. Feel free to make noises that match your exertion.

- **Do something generous.** Help someone, make a cup of tea for someone. Give someone a compliment. You cannot be in the World of One if you are noticing and assisting someone else.

- **Take action.** Do something that needs to get completed. Make a hard phone call, write a difficult email - do something that pushes you in that moment. Victims let the world happen to them; you are not a victim if you are doing something that will improve your situation.

- **Breathe.** Plan your next move, your next day. Get structure and control of the situation.

You've got this… You can get yourself out of the World of One.

PERSPECTIVE

perspective
/pəˈspɛktɪv/
noun

A particular attitude towards or way of regarding something; a point of view.[23]

I remember a particular football game that I watched when I was about 12 years old.

This was a special football game between the youth group at our Church (my dad was an Anglican Priest) and a team from Minda. Minda was a live-in support program for significantly intellectually disabled people. Dad's church was located next to Marion Shopping Centre not far from Brighton where Minda was located.

Every year Dad organised for the older kids from the youth group to play football against the older kids from Minda. It was a great day out. The game was played on the oval next to the church. It was a family picnic event. All the families of all the kids on both teams got together for this 'match'.

It was a great experience for all of the kids and their families. It broke down barriers, created a wonderful community spirit and was just a truly joyous day for everyone involved.

My dad told the youth group that he wanted the kids to play football, to give it their all and to have lots of fun and to remember there was only one rule. They had to let the kids from Minda win - just.

It was all about perspective. Of course, the youth group could beat the kids from Minda. That would be easy. But playing the game, being generous and making it an enjoyable event for the team from Minda and their families was the purpose of the day.

As the leader, you often know about your business and personal details of your individual team members. You know how the business is going financially, how your team members are performing. You have the inside

---

[23] Oxford English Dictionary

running on a lot of things.

You also see the world through the prism of a leader; the person who needs to keep this business or organisation moving forward. Your agenda will often be very different to that of one of your team members.

So it's important when dealing with personal staff issues that you be mindful of their perspective in that moment.

For example, Joe's contract may be up for renewal in four months' time. You know that Joe is performing fine and that you will be renewing his contract. You know that you have the funds to be able to do that and you are in the process of getting the paperwork drawn up.

Joe, however, doesn't know what is going on in your head. As every day creeps closer and closer to the end of his contract he gets more and more stressed. He needs this job to pay for his mortgage, he likes the people he is working with and he enjoys the work. But the boss isn't giving away any clues as to whether the contract is going to be extended and he is too scared to ask in case he jinxes the outcome. Silly, but that's how a lot of us think. He's hoping that no news is good news, but Joe isn't 100% sure - so he is stressed.

And because he is stressed he has started making some little mistakes. He's not concentrating properly. He's agitated and a bit snappy.

The boss, knowing Joe's circumstances, knowing the decision he is going to make can put Joe out of his misery sooner rather than later.

What the boss needs to do in this case is to look at the situation from Joe's perspective. He also needs to show some empathy and provide some clarity - so everyone can move on and get back to the job at hand.

Be Humble

Simon Sinek has a great presentation called 'Why Leaders Eat Last'[24]. He talks about humility and how leaders should care for their teams.

---

[24] Simon Sinek, 'Why Leaders Eat Last',
www.youtube.com/watch?v=ReRcHdeUG9Y

In my work as a mediator, I have often come across team conflicts where the team believes that the boss, the manager thinks that the team owes them. That the staff wouldn't have a job if not for the manager. That they should be grateful for their job, for the opportunities that the manager has bestowed on the lowly staff.

Often the staff think that they are working to line the CEO's pockets or to make them look good.

I have also heard CEOs and directors say that "this lot" should be grateful. That they are paid well and are well looked after.

There is resentment going both ways. This is not a thriving team because the perspective of the CEO or manager is that the team was created for their benefit.

It is not a team working towards a shared vision or a shared goal. It is a group of people employed for the purpose of stroking the ego of a manager. A leader brings people with them; managing a group of people to undertake a set of tasks is not in itself leadership.

The Port Adelaide Football Club has a very clear vision. It is: we exist to win premierships and to make our community proud. Whilst winning grand finals is hard to do, it is a vision that means that everyone involved in the club is working towards a shared vision where no one person is more important than anyone else.

The leaders of the club, the President, the CEO and the Coach have enormous responsibilities to hire well, choose good draft picks, spend their money wisely. But the players don't owe them anything because the perspective of the club is not about making one or two people look good; it's a whole of club responsibility to work towards winning a flag.

As soon as a coach or a CEO believes that any of the players owe them, they're in trouble.

The players have been selected for their skills and their commitment. They are paid well. In exchange for their high rates of remuneration they have to train hard, live in the public eye and perform each weekend of the football season. The club can't win a flag if the players don't play well. The club needs the players to meet their goals. So they need to look after the players by paying them appropriately, providing a safe work environment, setting firm and fair boundaries around performance and their contributions to the wider community and make them feel valued and appreciated.

Your team owes you nothing except a fair day's work. You owe your team everything because without them you can't progress your ideas, be successful in your field or increase your income.

People need people, and leaders need their team.

So you need to maintain a perspective that is generous, loving and kind.

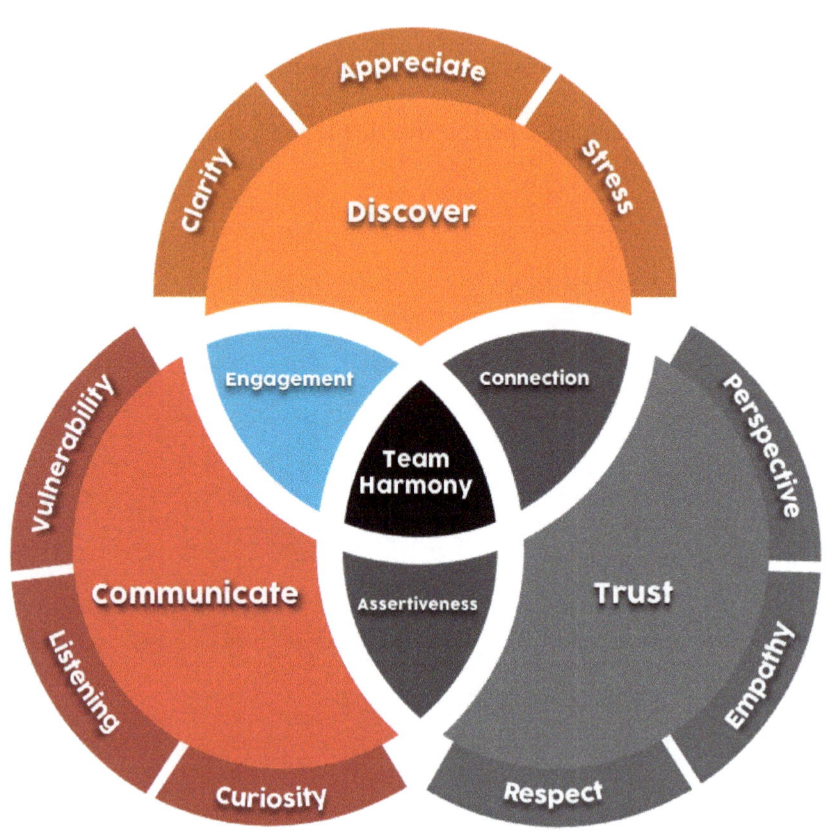

Appreciate
Clarity
Stress
Discover
Vulnerability
Engagement
Connection
Perspective
Team Harmony
Communicate
Assertiveness
Trust
Listening
Empathy
Curiosity
Respect

5   ENGAGEMENT

engagement
/ɪnˈɡeɪdʒm(ə)nt/
noun

To occupy or attract (someone's interest or attention)[25]

As leaders we are always looking for engagement from our teams, yet I hear all the time the age-old question, "How do I keep my team engaged?", "They arrive at 9am and they're packed up and ready to go at 4:30pm," or "Young people these days! They are so disengaged, all they want to do all day is look at their phones."

You get engagement when people want to be there. When it is not about the money but all about the play (doing what you are good at doing), feeling valued and respected and appreciated.

If we don't get that part of the puzzle right, we are left with a team that feels disengaged. They are not there; no-one is home. They might be going through the motions but they will do the bare minimum.

Productivity will be poor, mistakes will be made because care levels will be low and your business or organisation will face increased risk.

The other key plank to a productive workplace is to let people play. This doesn't mean bringing in a table tennis table (although they can be good fun); I mean when we let people use their skills to do a good job. In *Primed*

---

[25] Oxford English Dictionary

to Perform (2015), Doshi and McGregor describe how research clearly shows that what motivates people the most in the workplace is when they are engaging in an activity simply because they enjoy doing it. When people enjoy their work, then they want to be there. Turning up on Monday morning is no issue. Bring it on.

The other two motivators for people at work are Purpose and Potential. If people value the outcome of their work (purpose) or see the potential that they are on the right track and will one day be able to 'play' in this workplace - then they will be motivated to work. They will want to be there.

Money is not a direct motivator for people to want to work. The research shows over and over that staff are more likely to work harder and/or longer hours if their work is acknowledged. Paying bonuses and/or higher wages does not automatically translate to better results.

I have had first-hand experience of feeling disengaged. I have worked for an organisation where I have not felt valued or appreciated. Where the only time the manager contacted me was to tell me there was a problem.

This organisation showed gratitude once a year; at Christmas. As the organisation closed down for Christmas there would be a cheerful email with photos of the manager and a witty poem wishing us all a Merry Christmas and thanking us for our hard work throughout the year.

That was it. Come January it was back to criticism, complaints or deafening silence. It truly was a 'no news is good news' type of organisation.

My response to any criticism was "meh, if you don't care about me, I'm not sure why I would care about you."

I was not engaged; in fact, at times I was downright hostile.

The odd contact asking me how I was going or to see if there was anything they could do to help or give me clarity on would have been nice. But it didn't happen. Ever.

The more I disengaged, the more they looked for mistakes and problems. It was inevitable that I would move on. I felt like they hated me, that they were looking for opportunities to punish me all the time and they never talked to me to find out why my performance and productivity had nose-dived.

If you are the manager it is your responsibility to ensure that your team are engaged; not your team's responsibility to please you so that you will notice them.

If you want engagement, show people that you care about them. Don't take people for granted. Show appreciation, value their work, show an interest in them, be curious and listen to them.

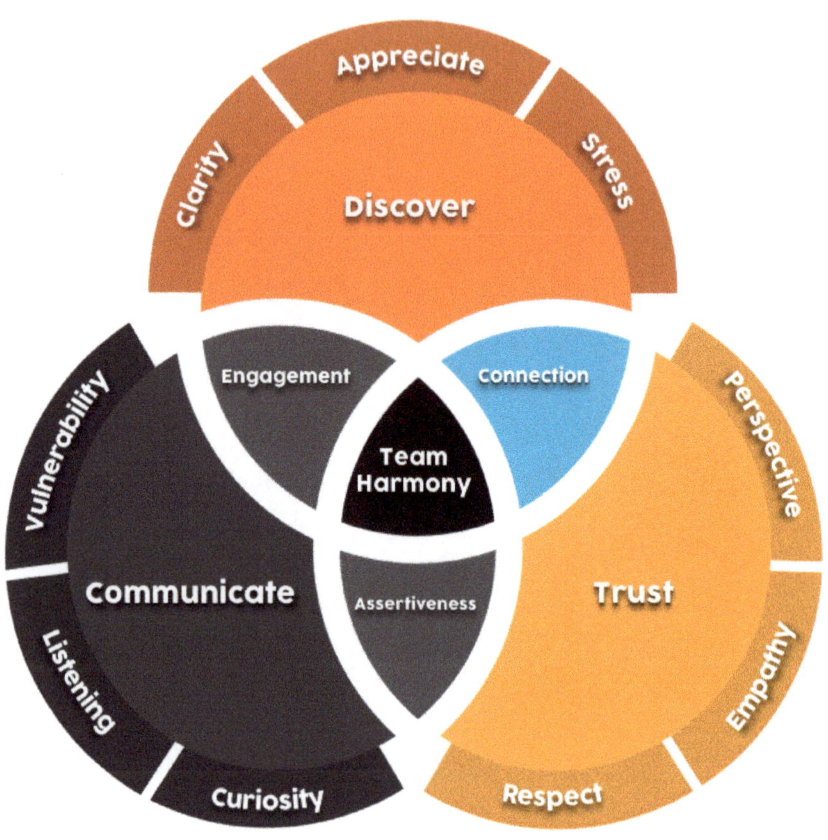

Appreciate
Clarity
Stress
Discover
Engagement
Connection
Vulnerability
Perspective
Team Harmony
Communicate
Trust
Assertiveness
Listening
Empathy
Curiosity
Respect

6   CONNECTION

connection
/kəˈnɛkʃ(ə)n/
noun

Bring together or into contact so that a real or notional link is established.[26]

I know the feeling of extraordinary connection. I felt it after a successful mediation process, on film sets, as the curtain closes on an extraordinary opening night performance and at the end of an AFL Grand Final.

It's that feeling when you feel like you are one with everyone around you; your tribe. It doesn't matter how different you are; that you don't all agree on a whole host of things or that tomorrow we all go in a different direction. But in that moment, right there and then there is a feeling of absolute and total connection.

My son Tom is an actor. In 2008, when he was only 10 years old, he was cast in the lead role of Chook in a film called Last Ride. He starred opposite Hugo Weaving and the film's director was a relative newcomer at that time, the wonderful Glendyn Ivin. It was a road movie filmed in the beautiful Flinders Ranges in South Australia. This team of cast and crew moved their base every week or so. Due to circumstances, they were forced to live in each other's pockets for about seven weeks.

As you can imagine they had their ups and downs. They partied hard some nights, broke bread together a lot, shared extraordinary experiences and had a lot of fun. And lots of things went wrong too, mistakes were made, scenes reshot, there were emergency dashes back to Adelaide for gear and crew members squabbled about stupid stuff. They were just an ordinary group of wonderful people hand-picked to

---

[26] Oxford English Dictionary

create this team who would make this particular movie.

My husband and I were there for the filming of the last scene. It was a night time scene at Port Gawler which meant that we were nearly home. Tom had not been home for seven weeks. The scene was of Tom and Hugo's characters going to sleep in the car that night. It was a scene of Hugo turning off the light in the car. Glendyn got them to do the scene probably one more time than was necessary; just because once it was done it meant that the filming part of the movie was over. Then he said that's a wrap. And it was over.

There were sparklers, whoops and hollers of joy, hugs and tears of joy and pride, hugs and tears of grief that this particular experience was over and everyone had to say goodbye. It was a hugely emotional and dynamic moment.

In that moment there was a total connection between everyone involved in the makimg of that film. It was profound.

People want to belong. It is a very powerful need. It is ranked third on Marlow's Hierarchy of Needs.

So sometimes, in organisations that are struggling or are really stressed, that sense of belonging is hard to come by or it results in silos. I have seen relatively small organisations that are operating with three or four small silos because of conflict between some of the middle managers.

The consequences for those organisations are dire. People do not communicate for fear of breaching the trust of a fellow silo member; opportunities are lost because there is no sharing of ideas and service delivery is usually negatively affected.

How do you create connections between people who are competing against each other for the boss' attention or bigger slices of the overall budget? How do you stop a popular kids' clique?

I accept that it is not easy but is something to constantly aspire to because the buck stops with you.

You work towards a common goal or vision that is bigger than the operating budget or someone's popularity.

If you are a sports team you focus on winning the flag. If you are a political party you focus on winning a seat or forming a Government. If you are a business you focus on a big lofty vision. A dollar amount or a certain outcome. You create a focus that is something that is the ultimate prize.

Many years ago I set up and ran the Child Support Unit at Legal Aid. We had a team of about thirteen staff. I used to tell the team that our goal was to be the best child support unit in the country. We would provide the best services, we would achieve the best outcomes for our clients. We would become a model for other states.

Now, there was no such thing as the best child support unit. There was no competition and no way of easily measuring how well we were performing against other units. The Commonwealth Government had data that they collated but we did not have access to that data.

But I used to tell the team on a regular basis that we were working towards being the best child support unit in the country. And we were. We constantly looked for ways to improve the way in which we provided services. We looked for ways to improve processes and how we worked together.

We had a great team. We were a team. There were no cliques. We had each other's backs. We were a force to be reckoned with. We were respected by our peers as being experts in child support. We had a very good relationship with Centrelink and the Child Support Agency, the relevant courts and the other various interest groups. And this meant we were able to provide very good outcomes for our clients and exceptional service delivery.

There will always be differences. There will always be people that don't get on within any team, but by focusing on big audacious goals and having a clear vision you will be able to unite your team so that they can sweat the small stuff.

Don't get stuck in the weeds; focus on the one thing that will unite your team and keep your focus up there.

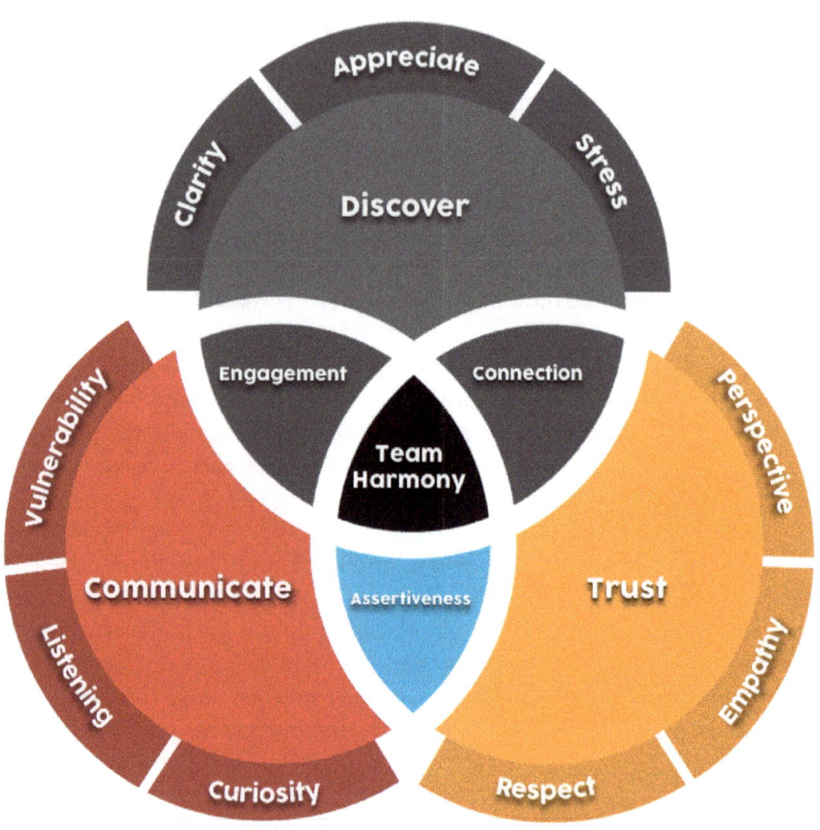

Appreciate
Clarity
Stress
Discover
Engagement
Connection
Vulnerability
Perspective
Team
Harmony
Communicate
Assertiveness
Trust
Listening
Empathy
Curiosity
Respect

7   ASSERTIVENESS

assertiveness
/əˈsəːtɪvnəs/
noun
   Behave or speak in a confident and forceful manner.[27]

One of my clients recently told me, "Kate, you are always in my head - every time I get annoyed with someone I think 'boundaries, boundaries, boundaries!'"

The Supernanny[28] is my hero. She calls out the parent's behaviour that is not okay and provides them with practical advice about how to look after their children better. She always expects parents to set boundaries. She holds them accountable.

As leaders, we need to have clarity about what is acceptable behaviour for our team and then hold our team to account for those behaviours. It is our role to manage the boundaries and set the tone for the rest of the team.

We need to be assertive and demonstrate how others should talk to each other and give feedback. If we won't take timely action when there is a problem, why should we expect the rest of the team to be assertive?

Being assertive does not mean being cruel or unfair. It is not about embarrassing people. It is just being confident and forceful when we need

---

[27] Oxford English Dictionary
[28] www.supernanny.co.uk

to be.

We can be confident when everyone knows the rules, when our vision and goals are clear. We can be forceful when we need to do so to look after ourselves or other members of the team.

If we see a member of our team being treated badly by a client or a stakeholder, then we have a responsibility to that team member to step in and call out the poor behaviour.

A leader I was working with talked about how this one client was often rude to the receptionist and would not take advice or listen to a junior member of the firm.

They invited the client into the office. They introduced the receptionist and the junior to the client.

They then told the client that if he continued to be disrespectful to their staff, then he would no longer be a good fit for their business.

The client huffed and puffed and decided that he no longer needed their services.

The client was cultured out. He was not a good fit for that business. He was disrespectful and rude.

The whole team recognised that the leadership team had their back. It set the tone for future clients. This is a firm that will not allow their staff to be treated poorly.

Being assertive also means that as a team you respect each other enough to deal with issues when they arise.

If someone does something that you are not comfortable with, there is an expectation that you, not your manager, will speak to the person privately about the matter at hand. You will do it in a curious and caring manner. But you will not hold a grudge and suffer; you will deal with it.

Brad likes tuna. Recently he has been bringing tuna to lunch every day. He eats his lunch at his desk and the entire office then stinks of tuna. Brad doesn't care because he likes tuna.

Sarah hates the smell of tuna. She sits next to Brad. He is her peer but they are working on different projects. She has tolerated Brad's tuna for about two months. She goes to her manager to complain about Brad eating tuna at his desk.

Sarah's manager says, maybe you should have a word with Brad if that is a problem for you.

Sarah is not happy with this response; she wants her manager to deal with it and get Brad to be more considerate.

Sarah, recognising that she has to deal with this issue, asks if she can speak to Brad privately.

Sarah is clearly embarrassed. She says that she feels very uncomfortable saying this but, well… "I really hate the smell of tuna and you are stinking up the office every day when you eat lunch at your desk and I can't stand it. Can you please eat your lunch somewhere else."

Brad goes a deep colour of red and says, "Oh, I'm so sorry, I didn't know you had a problem with the smell. I wasn't thinking. It's just that I'm working on a big project at the moment and I've been working through my lunch break. I'm sorry you don't like the smell of tuna.

"I will eat my lunch somewhere else. It will be good for me to have a break. Again I am so sorry. Thank you for telling me that there was a problem."

Sarah says okay and they go back to work.

Sarah feels a huge sense of relief. She has had the conversation. He didn't yell at her and he is going to do something about the problem.

Brad feels a bit embarrassed. He goes and takes the empty tin of tuna to the kitchen. He gets the Spray and Wipe and cleans his desk. He looks over at Sarah and says "Better?".

"Yes!" she says smiling.

Now, this might seem like a happily ever after story but sometimes it is that simple. Sometimes sorting out a problem is just one conversation; where the participants are polite and respectful.

If we start the conversation on the attack, chances are the conversation will go downhill from there.

If you are nervous about starting a potentially difficult or embarrassing conversation then tell the other person from the beginning that you feel uncomfortable or embarrassed. They will notice this and will recognise that this is not easy for you.

Focus on the behaviour you are uncomfortable with. Brad is not a bad person because he eats tuna. It's just that he hasn't thought about the consequences. It can be fixed if someone speaks up.

Speak your truth. Say what you need to say. Don't let people ignore the boundaries. Call out behaviour that is not appropriate. Do it in a curious and kind manner and it will be okay.

Because if you don't deal with these issues, if you let people exploit the situation, then you will start to resent them, you will diminish trust, engagement will dive and there will be little or no connection.

And people will gossip because no-one is dealing with the issues.

Rip the band-aid off and be assertive.

8   LEADERS WHO LEAD

lead
/liːd/
verb

> Cause (a person or animal) to go with one by holding them by the
> hand, a halter, a rope, etc. while moving forward.[29]

So there you have it. That is my roadmap for creating a team that thrives.
An energised, productive and connected team that feels loved and loves
back in return. A team where you all have each other's back and where you
all feel respected and valued.

We can't achieve that level of success without feeling all the feels. This
means being vulnerable and taking responsibility for anything we do that
may impact negatively on the team. We are human, we are fallible and we
will do things that upset some people, that accidentally infringes someone's
values or accidentally offends them.

We will get stressed and probably say and do things that we regret.

We will grieve when one of our team goes on to different pastures or if
one of our team goes through a difficult time.

We will celebrate when we are successful, big or small, and we will
thoroughly enjoy each other's company.

---

[29] Oxford English Dictionary

We will annoy each other sometimes, and we will miss each other at other times.

We will be like a family because that's what a thriving team is a lot like.

And that's okay.

I think the family analogy is really important because family is about life.

Firstly, I am not a fan of the term 'work-life balance'. I believe we just have life. I believe that what happens at works impacts on our home life and vice versa. They are different and separate but they are still connected by the people involved.

If I am going through a messy divorce, it will impact my work life. If I am facing a redundancy at work, it will affect my home life.

I also believe that if we are good leaders, then chances are we'll be good parents too. I think leadership is just like parenting. We want our kids to flourish, to succeed, to take risks and to be good people. Why wouldn't we want the same thing for our teams?

I believe that if you were to apply the same principles to your family (in particular to your relationship with your teenagers) you'd get great results too.

I learned early in life to find role models, in particular other mothers to help guide me to be a good person. I have learned a lot from all of my mentors who I handpicked when I was a child.

I also did a lot of therapy and consciously approached parenting as an experiment. I was usually mindful of the effect I was having on my kids. I think I did a pretty good job most of the time.

I have applied all of the elements of the model to my parenting over the years. I couldn't be prouder of my children and the young adults they have become.

I have also applied all of the elements of my model in my leadership roles with great success.

If you want your team to thrive, whether that team is your family or your work team; the best approach is to love them. Love them a lot. Love them even when it is hard to love them. You will be tested, you will be challenged, you will worry about them, you will celebrate with them. But the bottom line is relationships first and business second. When you look after the relationships everything else just falls into place.

Leadership is the process of taking people with you on a journey. It is not about doing everything for everyone; it is not about sitting back and letting everyone do the work for you. It is about being part of the whole and helping that group of people progress; move forward.

Leading your team is so much more exciting than just managing them. Leading a team is dynamic and powerful and rewarding and difficult and scary. It is an adventure that you go on together.

Leaders who lead take responsibility for the wellbeing of their team. The buck stops with them. The leader sets the tone of the team. The leader is responsible for ensuring that the team has clarity, knows where it is going, identifies the boundaries, holds themselves and the team accountable.

The leader takes responsibility for ensuring that all of the team are engaged and connected. It is not the team's responsibility to play nicely or to be kind to you; you set the rules with the team and you then hold them accountable for those agreed behaviours. The kind and thoughtful behaviour will come because of the environment you create.

The role of leader is one of great responsibility. A leader must have the courage to deal with issues that arise; to call out inappropriate behaviour, to make the hard call when it needs to be made.

Leaders who lead are humble, leave their egos at the door and have the courage to be vulnerable.

Leaders who lead love their teams. And their teams love them back.

Take care.

POSTSCRIPT

As you have probably worked out, family is incredibly important to me.

In closing, I want to pay tribute to my daughter Georgie who has taught me so much about love and life.

They say that you teach those things you need to learn most yourself. Those words resonate with me so much.

I teach people to slow down to speed up; to look after themselves to reduce their stress levels and I teach people to create boundaries so that everyone feels safe. These are all lessons that I have struggled with myself throughout my life.

But the greatest lesson of all is learning how to love someone who is sometimes hard to love. Whose behaviour sometimes pushes me to the limits. Who I care about deeply and who takes up so much of my brain space with worry and concern.

This book is dedicated to you, Georgie, for all of the incredible lessons you have taught me.

Here is my blog to celebrate Georgie's birthday in April 2018.

Today is Georgie's birthday. Georgie is my daughter. She is a wonderful young adult in the prime of her life.

Georgie has taught me more about love than anyone else in my life.

Georgie has, over the years, pushed my buttons in ways that no-one else ever has.

I have spent an extraordinary amount of time worrying about her; being frustrated with her and also for her.

We have fought a lot. There have been so many tears. We've had to apologise to each other a lot.

We've gone in to bat for each other. Celebrated each other's successes.

We've gone on long long walks and barely spoken.

We've holidayed together overseas and not seen the same things.

We've been disappointed in each other. Not understood each other.

We have joyously climbed the Sydney Harbour Bridge together.

We've spent hours in doctor's surgeries and hospital together.

We have sold her art together.

We have lived and loved and cried and experienced a lot of life together.

But what has made it special and sometimes so incredibly challenging is that Georgie has Asperger's.

She doesn't see or experience the world the way I do.

She challenges the way I think and experience life all the time. It is such a wonderful gift and I am so grateful to her for helping me and our entire family be so more tolerant of difference.

Thank you George. I love you.

ACKNOWLEDGEMENTS

I wrote this book in a relatively short period of time, but it was a long time in the making. I have learned from and honed my skills over many, many years and I am very grateful to all the people I have worked for and worked with for all the life lessons I have learned.

I would also like to thank a number of people who have cheered me on, provided me with valuable advice or who have lived through this experience of book writing with me.

I would like to thank my business coaches and mentors for their wise counsel, Cheryll Hill, Brett Odgers, John Munro and Bram Lagrou. You have all been instrumental in one way or the other to my journey in the last two years. I value our chats, your wise counsel, your enthusiasm and constantly encouraging me to keep moving.

To one of my oldest friends Cathy Faulkner, who also happens to be my long-suffering accountant, thank you for sticking with me and for your guidance.

To Bel Ryan, art therapist, you are a genius and a dear friend. I have dealt with a lot of 'stuff' in the last twelve months. I trust you implicitly and your curiosity and ability to ask the right question is profound. I have learned so much about myself through our journey; thank you for challenging me and helping me find myself.

To my favourite good witch and remedial massage therapist, Valerie Shearing, thank you for your intuition and support. You are a valued friend and your generosity is profound.

To my good friend Chris Edgar, thank you for believing in me and constantly putting ideas in my head. You constantly demonstrate the power of loving and kind leadership. You are a respected leader and mentor to many.

To all of my wonderful and cherished family - thank you. This journey started when I was in my teens when my dad introduced me to psychotherapy; his third career. The one he took up to work out how to look after my mum. As a result of Dad's passion for Gestalt Therapy and Transactional Analysis, I developed a keen and intense interest in how people tick; why and how we end up in difficult conflict situations and the benefits of owning and taking responsibility for how we react to situations, whether that be good or bad.

I made a very definite decision at about the age of 18 years old that I would not parent like my parents. They were not bad people, but they were dealing with a lot of their own issues and they were so stressed throughout most of my childhood that they couldn't parent well.

Despite my best efforts to parent better than my parents, I still made a lot of mistakes.

I left home at 17 years old and ended up in a long-term relationship at the ripe old age of 18 years and 6 months. I was a baby and in all honesty, the main thing that my first husband and I had in common was that we came from families that were struggling; both our families had a lot of issues to deal with.

The wheels of our relationship pretty much fell off when we became parents.

Despite this, we stayed together for a number of years and had three extraordinary children.

It's hard to be a great parent when you are in a not-so-great relationship and feeling stressed all the time.

Unsurprisingly that relationship did not last which was for the best.

I have been with my beloved Gus for nearly 20 years. All of our children have grown up and we are empty nesters with a house that is always full of family visiting from somewhere or coming for dinner, or staying over because our house is warmer or cooler than theirs.

Gus and I love being parents. It is our number one topic of conversation and we both recognise that it is the hardest job in the world and the most rewarding.

I think the biggest lesson I have learned from my family is that you cannot separate work from home. They both influence each other enormously. Which is why it is so important that we create teams that thrive and workplaces that are exciting and rewarding. Stress is a killer; literally. It nearly killed me. I let work and life get to me; I didn't have boundaries, I didn't look after myself. I was pleasing, controlling and unhappy. Dealing with my serious health issues of 2013 and 2014 changed my life. I got my life back and my relationships with my family blossomed.

So this book is important to me because family is so important to me.

Finally, I want to say a special thank you to both my husband Gus (Graham Russell) and my daughter Lucy Russell Byrne.

Gus is my rock. He is calm, where I am a bit manic. He thinks a lot (whilst I tend to react). He is generous, kind and a bit fanatical. He barracks for Port Adelaide and so it follows that the entire family barracks for Port Adelaide. He is a natural leader and we all follow him. He also edits most of our work and makes sound suggestions. He is adored by our entire family. He went on the health journey with me. When I stopped drinking, he stopped drinking. When I needed to start exercising, he came on the walks with me. We both usually get up at stupid o'clock every day to do some exercise. He is a rock and I feel blessed to share my life with him.

And Lucy has been my right hand since she was eight years old when my first husband and I separated. At that time I was a single parent with an 8-year-old, a 6-year-old with disabilities and a brand new baby. Lucy and I were the team. She would look after one child and I would look after the other. We did a great job.

We have been a great team ever since. We help each other out all the time. She has edited and published this book for me. She has taught me about social media, she uses her creativity to turn my words into art. I cannot thank Lucy enough for her extraordinary contribution to my life and my work.

Family is everything to me. Family is possibly everything to you too.

Look after your team, reduce stress in your workplace, be generous and empathetic with your people. Take responsibility for your team and share your team's success. Have the courage to do the hard things and call out inappropriate behaviour when you see it.

Love your team and your family will be forever grateful.

ABOUT THE AUTHOR

Kate Russell is a coach and trainer who helps leaders create conflict resilient teams and take their teams from good to great.

She is an accredited mediator (Resolution Institute) and trained conflict management coach (CINERGY ™) with over twenty-five years' experience working with people and teams dealing with conflict.

Kate believes that prevention is better than cure. If we look after our team, appreciate and trust them, and provide a safe working environment, then we will reap the rewards.

Kate is able to help more leaders in professional services firms and their teams thrive by providing online training and coaching.

Kate has created a number of training tools which provide leaders with a step by step process to build greater engagement and connection within their teams. She also runs on-line small coaching groups in a safe, confidential environment so that your questions get answered by her and you receive ongoing support.